This publication was developed through funding from the National Institute of Corrections, U.S. Department of Justice. Points of view stated in this publication are those of the authors and do not necessarily represent the official position or policies of the U.S. Department of Justice or the National Institute of Corrections.

# CONTENTS

Message From the Director .................................................. vii
Foreword .................................................................. ix
Acknowledgments ........................................................... xi
Commentary ............................................................... xiii
Introduction ............................................................. xvii

**Chapter 1.** How Motivational Interviewing Fits In
With Evidence-Based Practice ............................................... 1
    What Is the Goal of Supervision? ....................................... 2
    What Is Evidence-Based Practice? ....................................... 2
        Where Did Evidence-Based Practice Come From? ..................... 2
        Why Does Evidence-Based Practice Matter? ......................... 4
    What Are the Principles of Effective Interventions? .................... 5
        Risk ............................................................. 6
        Criminogenic Needs ............................................... 6
        Responsivity ..................................................... 8
    How Does Motivational Interviewing Fit in With Evidence-Based Practice? ..... 9

**Chapter 2.** How and Why People Change ................................... 11
    Old Assumptions About Motivation ...................................... 11
    New Findings on Motivation ............................................ 12
    How People Change ..................................................... 14
    Why People Change ..................................................... 16

**Chapter 3.** The Motivational Interviewing Style ......................... 21
    What Is Motivational Interviewing? .................................... 21
    What Are the Basic Assumptions of Motivational Interviewing? .......... 23
    How Does Motivational Interviewing Facilitate Change? ................. 24
        It Reduces Resistance ........................................... 24
        It Raises Discrepancy ........................................... 25
        It Elicits Change Talk .......................................... 25
    For Whom Is Motivational Interviewing Best Suited? .................... 27

# CONTENTS

**Chapter 4.** Preparing for Change .................................... 29
    Ask Open-Ended Questions ........................................ 29
    Affirm Positive Talk and Behavior ................................. 33
    Reflect What You Are Hearing or Seeing ............................ 36
    Summarize What Has Been Said .................................... 41
    An Example: Good Things and Not-So-Good Things .................... 42
    Exercise: Rolling with Resistance ................................. 47
    Useful Questions for Motivational Interviews ...................... 48
    Useful Statements for Motivational Interviews ..................... 49

**Chapter 5.** Building Motivation for Change ........................... 51
    Pick a Focus .................................................... 51
    Look For and Emphasize Things That Motivate ....................... 52
        Ask Questions That Raise Interest ............................ 52
        Follow Up on Productive Talk ................................. 53
        Use Forward-Focused Questions ................................ 56
        Ask Scaled (Rather Than Yes/No) Questions .................... 57
    Strengthen Commitment To Change ................................... 60
        Ask an Action Question ....................................... 61
        Give Advice Without Telling What To Do ....................... 61
        Help Connect Talk to Action .................................. 64
    Exercise: Asking Good Questions ................................... 67
    Communication Examples ............................................ 68

**Chapter 6.** Navigating Tough Times: Working With Deception,
Violations, and Sanctions ............................................. 69
    Lying and Deception ............................................. 69
        Why Do People Lie? ........................................... 69
        What Can Be Done About It? ................................... 71
    Addressing Violations and Sanctions ............................... 71
        Explain the Dual Role ........................................ 71
        Be Clear About the Sanctions ................................. 72
        Address Behavior With an "Even Keel" Attitude ................ 72
    When the Offender Denies the Initial Offense ...................... 74

**Chapter 7.** From Start to Finish: Putting Motivational
Interviewing Into Practice ............................................ 77
    Moving From Motivation to Commitment .............................. 77
    Adapting Motivational Interviewing to Different Kinds of Interviews ......... 80

## CONTENTS

    The First Meeting ............................................... 80
    Motivational Interviewing and the Case-Planning Interview .............. 82
    Motivational Interviewing and Routine Meetings ...................... 84
    Motivational Interviewing and the Postviolation Interview .............. 88
Managing Time Constraints ........................................... 89

References ....................................................... 91
About the Authors ................................................. 99

## List of Exhibits

Exhibit 1–1. Pendulum Swings in Correctional Policy ..................... 3
Exhibit 2–1. Short-Term Markers of Long-Term Change ................... 13
Exhibit 2–2. The Stages of Change ..................................... 14
Exhibit 2–3. Issues and Strategies in the Stages of Change................. 15
Exhibit 2–4. Motivational Continuum .................................. 17
Exhibit 3–1. Probability of Behavior Change ............................ 23
Exhibit 3–2. Agent Confrontation and Offender Resistance ................ 24
Exhibit 3–3. Movement Along the Motivational Continuum................ 26
Exhibit 3–4. Flow of Change Talk ..................................... 27
Exhibit 4–1. Closed Versus Open-Ended Questions ...................... 30
Exhibit 4–2. Rolling With Resistance .................................. 40
Exhibit 5–1. Transforming Backward-Focused to Forward-Focused Questions .. 56
Exhibit 5–2. Transforming Yes/No Questions to Scaled Questions ............ 57
Exhibit 5–3. Importance and Confidence Rulers ......................... 58
Exhibit 5–4. Two Phases of Motivation ................................. 61
Exhibit 5–5. Responses That Facilitate Rather Than Dictate Solutions......... 63

# MESSAGE FROM THE DIRECTOR

The corrections field, and community corrections in particular, has long experienced tensions between its two main missions, protecting public safety and rehabilitating offenders. Treatment-oriented strategies that had as their goal the reintegration of offenders into society have contended with deterrence-oriented strategies based on apparent findings that "nothing works" in treating offenders. In recent years, the development and application of evidence-based practices (EBP)—practices informed by the results of scientific research and shown to increase public safety and reduce recidivism—have had a profound and positive impact on the corrections field. More thorough scientific analysis of both treatment- and deterrence-oriented programs has shown that many programs that emphasized motivation and behavior change over punishment have been successful in reducing crime rates among offenders. The National Institute of Corrections (NIC), through its sponsorship of studies and its training programs, has been a leader in the movement toward EBP in the corrections field and an advocate of more rigorous scientific analysis of programs for offenders.

One promising evidence-based practice for motivating offenders and fostering positive behavioral changes is motivational interviewing (MI). MI, which was first developed in the addiction treatment field, is now being applied widely and with positive results in corrections, particularly in probation and parole. The principle behind MI is that by listening to offenders and following up on the positive aspects of their speech and thinking, corrections professionals can help increase offenders' motivation to make positive changes in their lives that will reduce their likelihood of reoffending.

This publication, *Motivating Offenders To Change: A Guide for Probation and Parole,* provides probation and parole officers and other correctional professionals with both a solid grounding in the principles behind MI and a practical guide for applying these principles in their everyday dealings with offenders. Through numerous examples of questions, sample dialogues, and exercises, it presents techniques for interacting with offenders at all stages of supervision and at varying levels of commitment to positive change. In addition, it recognizes that deception, resistance to change, and relapse into criminal behaviors are realities for many offenders, and sets forth strategies for dealing with those issues that avoid unproductive confrontation with the offender.

# MESSAGE FROM THE DIRECTOR

*Motivating Offenders To Change* is intended as an orientation tool for new probation and parole professionals, a classroom aid for supervisors and trainers, and a self-study resource for individual officers. Our hope is that the guide will not only promote the use of MI, but also will help empower probation and parole officers and other correctional professionals to act as positive influences for change in the lives of the offenders they supervise.

**Morris L. Thigpen, Sr.**
*Director*
National Institute of Corrections

# FOREWORD

*Motivating Offenders To Change: A Guide for Probation and Parole* provides the reader with a valuable primer on the tenets of motivational interviewing. The authors lay out the foundations of motivational interviewing and give examples of how it can be implemented. The authors have taken care to present information in an easily digestible and commonsense style. They provide guidance while remaining cognizant of the resource and time challenges faced by probation and parole staff. The book serves as a valuable prerequisite and aid to training in the use of this effective technique for facilitating positive offender change.

Although some probation and parole staff may be unfamiliar with motivational interviewing, it is not a new approach. Motivational interviewing grew out of the substance abuse and addiction treatment fields in the 1980s. At that time, research began to show that the widely accepted confrontational approaches to dealing with addicts simply were not successful. As a result, treatment professionals began to implement strategies that recognized and encouraged autonomy, self-determination, and positive reinforcement. Their success rates began to climb. In the past 25 years, motivational interviewing has been adapted to the medical and social service fields and has now proven to be a significant tool for facilitating positive behavior change in persons with a range of addictions and others seeking to make positive changes in their lives.

This guide reminds officers that their interactions with offenders have a pivotal role in determining subsequent behavior. If criminal justice professionals rely solely on punishment and incarceration—or the threat of punishment and incarceration—they neglect the greater part of their contribution. The social and financial costs associated with repeat offender incarceration are simply too high to ignore evidence-based strategies like motivational interviewing. Treating offenders in a harsh, rigid manner may look good politically, but it does not net the results that society deserves. Deterrence may work in the short term, but empowering offenders to change will work in the long term.

The audience of the guide is intentionally broad: probation and parole officers and supervisors, juvenile officers, training directors, counselors, and others who work in adult and youth justice settings. Departments might distribute all or portions of the book as part of an orientation for new officers or before or after training in motivational interviewing, or they may simply make the guide available as a resource to those who want to improve their skills. Supervisors, in particular, may want to use this guide to become familiar with the techniques of motivational interviewing, instruct staff in specific interviewing skills, and provide ongoing supervision and quality control.

For readers who entered the field of criminal or juvenile justice believing that people can change and wanting to have a positive impact, this book should provide hope and confidence. For those who came into the field believing that behavior change is unlikely and that the primary role of an officer is to enforce conditions of supervision through rigid monitoring and punishment, this book may offer an alternative approach to supervision. Probation and parole staff can indeed have a larger role than simply enforcing conditions; they can be the impetus for positive change that increases long-term public safety.

**Carl R. Wicklund**
American Probation and
Parole Association

# ACKNOWLEDGMENTS

A number of individuals helped form this book. First, the authors owe a great debt, both personally and professionally, to William Miller and Stephen Rollnick, the developers of the motivational interviewing (MI) approach. The authors also acknowledge the contributions of the Motivational Interviewing Network of Trainers, who have generously shared ideas about how best to present training material.

There were also a number of individuals who provided feedback on earlier sections of the monograph. In particular, Francis Cullen and Patricia Harris provided feedback on evidence-based practice; Melissa Cahill, Mike Donoho, Robert Rhode, and Pam Smithstan provided feedback on theories of motivation and behavior change; Cathy Cole, Joel Ginsberg, and Kathyleen Tomlin provided feedback on MI theory; Stephen Brazill, Grant Corbett, Stephen Emslie, Tad Gorske, Byron McIntyre, and Lyn Williams provided feedback on MI practice; and Brad Bogue, Glenn Homolka, Dee Dee Stout, Chuck Sweetman, and Dub Wright provided feedback on adapting MI to probation settings. Amanda Vader provided assistance with editing and referencing. These professionals read and commented on large portions of the original draft, and their comments contributed greatly to the final product.

The National Institute of Corrections (NIC) provided funding for the guide, and the University of Texas School of Public Health supported Dr. Walters's time while he worked on it. Dot Faust, Michael Guevara, and Georgette Walsh with NIC guided the draft into a final product, and were a pleasure to work with.

Finally, I would like to thank the Communications staff at Lockheed Martin for their work in editing, designing, and producing the printed publication. Brian Higgins and Janet McNaughton provided clear editing that enhanced the readability of the guide. Denise Collins and Rita Harding created an open design that kept to the overall spirit of the product, and Misae Walko and Huey Chang ably executed the layout.

**Scott Walters, Ph.D.**
University of Texas School of Public Health

# COMMENTARY

## Pros and Cons: Reflections on Motivational Interviewing in Correctional Settings

### William Miller, Ph.D.

More than a decade ago, applications of motivational interviewing broke out of the addiction field and have been spreading into new and interesting areas: cardiovascular rehabilitation, diabetes management, family preservation, pain management, public health interventions, and the prevention of HIV infection. The most recent surge of interest, in North America at least, is coming from a field where I least expected it: the criminal justice system. We are receiving calls for training from jails and prisons, courts, probation and parole departments, community corrections, diversion and pre-release programs.

At first I was curious as to why this is happening. Now my sense is, "Why not?" I realize, too, that my own initial surprise and reluctance were based on inaccurate stereotypes. "Lock 'em up and throw away the key" is rather opposite to the perspective that we seek to promote in MI. Yet the limitations of punishment and imprisonment are apparent to no one more than to those who work in correctional systems every day. More than the vast majority, who never set foot behind bars, they know first-hand that what American society is doing is simply not working. They understand well the passionate plea made in Karl Menninger's *The Crime of Punishment*. In training probation officers this year I met a group of profoundly patient and compassionate professionals who were doing their best, not to exact society's revenge, but to change behavior. Far from media fantasies of good guys versus bad guys, they work daily with the real people who are sentenced to temporarily restricted freedom.

I am, on reflection, particularly thankful that there seems to be interest and openness to a personally respectful MI approach within criminal justice settings. "Prisoners" and "criminals" are among society's most despised and rejected members. In the name of justice, they are routinely subjected in prisons to isolation, crowding, dehumanization, humiliation, terror, drug abuse, privation, and physical and sexual violence. These conditions are widely known (even as a subject of TV comedian

---

Reprinted with permission from the *Motivational Interviewing Newsletter: Updates, Education and Training (MINUET)* (6)1: 2–3, 1999.

## COMMENTARY

monologues) and are tolerated, as if they were "good for" offenders and for society. Among nations, America has one of the world's highest rates of incarcerated citizens, ranking with the most oppressive societies; yet the building of new prisons remains a growth industry.

It reminds me of how things once were in the addiction treatment field in the United States. The boot camp atmosphere of Synanon. The in-your-face screaming of insults and obscenities. Denial busting. The hot seat, "tearing them down to build them up." The surprise confrontational meetings that could feature on the front page of the *Wall Street Journal,* as exemplary practice, a physician shouting at an executive, "Shut up and listen! Alcoholics are liars, and we don't want to hear what you have to say!" The "family week" where people were told they had the fatal disease of co-dependency by virtue of being related to an alcoholic, and that they were thereby out of touch with reality and required treatment. It seems like a bad dream now, but it was very common just two decades ago. There are far too many places where these things still occur.

Something happened in the addiction field. A punitive, moralistic, and arrogant stance that was common in U.S. treatment twenty years ago has given way to a much more respectful and collaborative approach. I'm not sure that motivational interviewing had anything to do with it, but the field's amazing receptiveness to MI is at least a reflection of this profound change. In the 1970s it was acceptable, even laudable, to abuse "alcoholics" and "drug addicts" because it was good for them, it was what they needed, the only way to get through to them. It's no surprise, given this treatment, that there arose the impression that defensiveness is a natural concomitant of substance use disorders. Something happened. In a relatively short period of time, treatment has changed.

Is it too much to hope, then, that the field of corrections could see a similarly major change in the next twenty years? Offenders are the last major group in our society whom it is generally acceptable to abuse because they "need" and "deserve" it—because it is good for them and for society, and is "the only language they can understand." All evidence to the contrary, we collectively imagine somehow that it makes them better, and makes us a safer and more just society.

What would happen if motivational interviewing became a routine part of the training of correctional workers? What if large numbers of volunteers were trained to go into prisons and listen to offenders in this way? How would it affect outcomes if offenders were generally seen as preparing for change (like those entering treatment), rather than as less-than-human cons? What if we assumed that the central purpose of correctional systems is not to enact vengeance, but to change behavior? I know it is possible. Remarkable changes sometimes happen, in people and in systems, in a relatively short period of time. There are so many points in societal justice systems where motivational interviewing could be tried. Ed Bernstein, Morris Chafetz, Damaris Rohsenow and others have offered brief empathic interventions to people in hospital emergency rooms, in the midst of crisis. What if, upon arrest, someone besides a lawyer met with people at the police station, just to listen in an MI style? Follow them through the system: in the jail, meeting with their lawyer, pre-trial, pre-sentencing, post-sentencing, on probation, beginning and during incarceration, on work release, pre-parole, post-release, before and after the end of a term of sentence. There are so many points in the system where motivational interviewing could be done. One can imagine many obstacles and objections. Yet it is possible. Motivational interviewers belong behind bars.

Perhaps, just perhaps, in twenty years' time we will look back on today's criminal justice practices and ask in disbelief, "How could it ever have been so?" Who in the addiction field imagined, twenty years ago, that we would be looking back disapprovingly, even shamefully at the confrontational models of the 1970s? These days when I begin talks with my old slides on the confrontation-of-denial model, even U.S. audiences sometimes refuse to believe that these things would ever actually be done in practice, and they accuse me of manufacturing a straw man. Who would have believed it? The straw man is dancing!

# INTRODUCTION

Motivational interviewing (MI) is an evidence-based practice that corrections professionals are now using to encourage positive behavior change in offenders. The push toward evidence-based practices is partially in response to research suggesting that effective correctional programs share similar characteristics as well as evidence from other areas that brief interactions can significantly influence offender outcomes. In this effort, MI offers an empirically supported approach for communicating with offenders about compliance and behavior change.

## Whom the Guide Is For

This guide is designed to serve as an MI primer and coaching tool for probation and parole officers and supervisors. It includes background information on evidence-based practices and behavior change theory and instructions and examples for using MI in correctional settings. Most of the examples focus on probation and parole officer interactions with offenders, though many of the interviewing skills will also be useful for counselors, social workers, court officers, and others who work in youth and adult correctional settings. The guide is designed to be used as part of the initial orientation for new officers, as part of continuing education for more seasoned officers, and as a resource for any who are interested in the topic.

## How the Guide Is Organized

The guide has seven chapters. Early chapters provide background on evidence-based practices and behavior change theory; later chapters give the rationale and specific instructions and examples for implementing MI as part of different interactions with probationers and parolees.

Chapter 1, "How Motivational Interviewing Fits In With Evidence-Based Practice," explains the logic of evidence-based practice, offers a brief history of the tension between the punitive and rehabilitative approaches to interacting with offenders, and explores MI's role in evidence-based practice.

Chapter 2, "How and Why People Change," illustrates the processes individuals go through before, during, and after making behavior changes. The chapter introduces the Stages of Change model and suggests factors that make change more likely.

Chapter 3, "The Motivational Interviewing Style," gives the rationale for the MI approach. It talks about the roles of empathy, resistance, discrepancy, and self-efficacy, and shows why these elements are pivotal to encouraging change.

Chapter 4, "Preparing for Change," talks about techniques that are used during the initial stages of change. The chapter shows how open and closed questions, reflections, affirmations, and summaries help establish rapport, gather information, and engage the offender in the change process.

Chapter 5, "Building Motivation for Change," suggests ways to use questions and statements strategically to build motivation for change and connect talk to action.

Chapter 6, "Navigating Tough Times: Working With Deception, Violations, and Sanctions," talks about ways to handle situations that involve deception. The chapter explains why people may lie, how to address these issues, and how to address violations and sanctions without leaving a motivational style.

Chapter 7, "From Start to Finish: Putting Motivational Interviewing Into Practice," describes strategies for using MI throughout the supervision period. The chapter details the most effective ways to incorporate MI into the initial interview, case planning, routine visits, and postviolation interviews.

Two final notes about language: In referring to persons on probation, this guide alternates between "person" and "offender." The authors recognize that these terms may fall short; "person" may not be descriptive enough while "offender" captures only the aspect of how the person entered the system. However, the authors could not identify another term that captured what we were looking for—someone who is unfolding or changing over time, while still under correctional supervision.

This guide also uses the masculine pronoun "he" to refer to offenders. The authors are, of course, aware that there are many female probationers, but because most probationers are male, early readers said that it improved readability to use a single pronoun. When referring to the probation or parole officer, or *agent*, the guide uses "he or she." Again for readability, the guide refers to "agents" when discussing the professionals who deal with offenders on a day-to-day basis. This term allows for easy distinction from "offender" in the many dialogue excerpts that illustrate MI techniques. The term "agent" also reflects that in addition to probation and parole officers, many of the skills are applicable to counselors, social workers, and others who work in the adult and youth justice systems. Where the context specifically relates to probation and parole officers, however, the term officer is used. The authors encourage readers to adapt the skills as is appropriate to the setting.

CHAPTER 1

# How Motivational Interviewing Fits In With Evidence-Based Practice

A probation officer receives two new cases this week. The first case, Anna, is a 27-year-old mother of two. She received a 6-month supervision period for passing bad checks. She was in trouble with the law once before. One year ago, the neighbors at her apartment complex called the police to report a domestic disturbance. When the police arrived, they found a small amount of methamphetamines. Anna's boyfriend brandished a weapon at police officers and was subsequently sentenced to 6 months in the county jail. The court dismissed Anna's case after she successfully completed a 60-day inpatient drug treatment. She currently receives public assistance and her living and employment situations are unstable. There is no evidence of recent drug use. Anna is seen as a low- to medium-risk offender.

The second case, Bill, is a 43-year-old man with a substantial history of drug use and violence. He is under supervision for driving while intoxicated (DWI) and recently served a short jail sentence for assaulting a bartender who refused to serve him. The bar and bartender have also filed a civil case against Bill for injuries and damages sustained during the assault. Bill has been in and out of various electrician jobs over the past few years and his current employment status is unclear. With the exception of a brother who lives in another state, Bill is estranged from his family. Results of a urinalysis show that he used cocaine and marijuana as recently as 1 week ago. Although Bill has been referred to several drug treatment programs, he has not had a significant period of sobriety in several years. Bill is seen as a medium- to high-risk offender because of his personal and family history of criminal behavior.

To some extent, departmental policy and assessment results will guide the supervision process. However, the probation officer will also make a number of decisions based on his or her personal beliefs about what approach will be most effective with these offenders. How will the probation officer speak to these offenders? How similarly should the two be treated? How much time will be spent on monitoring progress versus talking about rehabilitation?

## What Is the Goal of Supervision?

The mission statements of most corrections agencies emphasize two main tasks: holding offenders accountable to conditions (compliance), and encouraging positive behavior change (rehabilitation). Though these two tasks may seem self-evident, a quick look at the history of corrections shows that the field has emphasized different goals at different times. These two tasks have frequently been at odds with one another, and even today, the tension between them can be hard to manage. This chapter begins with a look at the history of community corrections. It then talks about why evidence-based practice might matter to supervision staff. Finally, it explains how motivational interviewing (MI) fits in with the current goals of supervision.

## What Is Evidence-Based Practice?

Criminal justice systems engage in a wide range of activities to stop offenders from committing crimes, but not all those activities are equally successful. Programs can make behavior better, worse, or have no effect. For a treatment or program to be called evidence based, its effectiveness must be substantiated by a measurable outcome (e.g., decreased recidivism, increased public safety). In corrections, evidence-based practice (EBP) refers to programs that have been shown to reduce recidivism (Andrews and Bonta, 2003; Miller, Zweben, and Johnson, 2005). EBP moves beyond the older "best practices" models that were based on the collective experience of the field in that it emphasizes the results of scientific research.

### Where Did Evidence-Based Practice Come From?

Scientific evidence has not always guided correctional practices (Cullen and Gendreau, 2001). In fact, until recently, community corrections practice was most often guided by whatever approach an agent was trained in or preferred. Two issues have discouraged agents from looking closely at their interactions with offenders. First, most agents simply assumed that what they did worked, and so had little incentive to look further. Second, performance measures for correctional officers have traditionally been linked to the technical aspects of the job (e.g., writing reports, court/board appearances, collection of fees) rather than to offender outcomes. Practice results could evade attention because the agent could always blame the offender for a poor outcome.

Historically, the corrections field has taken two basic approaches to changing offender behavior (McGuire, 2002):

- **Deterrence strategies** use negative consequences to reduce undesirable behaviors. Methods include incarceration, punitive sanctions (e.g., fines, community restraints, electronic surveillance), and "get tough" programs that teach offenders structure and discipline (e.g., boot camps, wilderness programs).

- **Constructional strategies** emphasize reducing undesirable behavior through teaching new skills and providing opportunities to use the new skills. Methods include increasing a person's opportunities and capacity for positive actions (e.g., skills training, education, employment) or helping the person succeed at some new behavior (e.g., drug treatment).

Three major shifts in correctional philosophy have occurred over the last 100 years. During some periods, corrections professionals have emphasized deterrence strategies; during others, they have relied more on treatment and constructional strategies. No period has emphasized one strategy alone; the difference has been in the degree to which they relied on one or the other. Exhibit 1–1 summarizes the major pendulum swings in corrections (Cullen and Gendreau, 2001).

**Exhibit 1–1.** Pendulum Swings in Correctional Policy

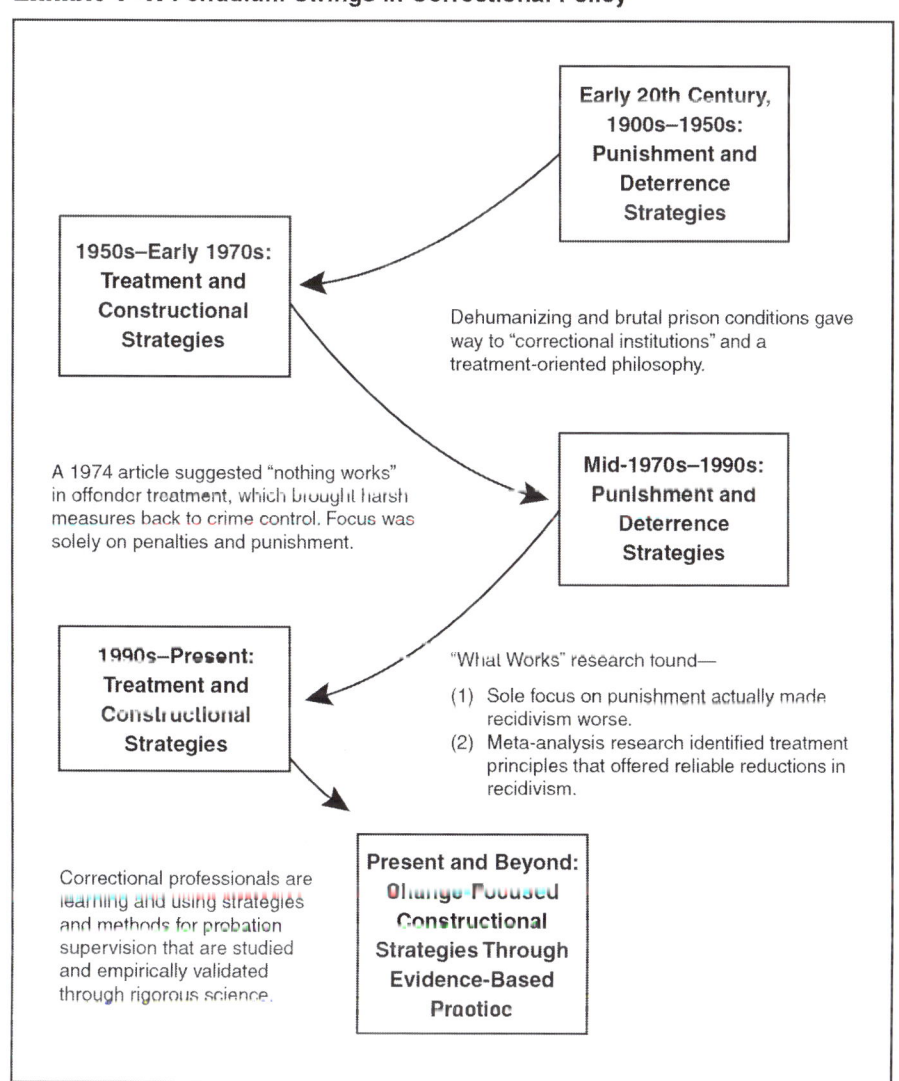

CHAPTER 1

In the early 1900s, the corrections field began to use treatment principles after many years of dehumanizing and brutal prison conditions. A rehabilitation approach flourished in the 1950s and 1960s. In fact, constructional strategies were so common that it was taken for granted that the purpose of state intervention was to rehabilitate offenders. A second pendulum swing in the mid-1970s back to punishment happened because of prisoner complaints about arbitrary probation and parole decisions and a public outcry against large increases in crime. Rehabilitation-oriented policies were blamed for much of the trouble. This position was reflected in a 1974 literature review (Lipton, Martinson, and Wilks, 1975; Martinson, 1974) that suggested "nothing worked" in offender treatment. This pessimistic view began to reverberate across the field of criminology until treatment was considered synonymous with coddling offenders. The new belief was that criminals needed to be held strictly accountable for their crimes and that treatment only served to undermine personal accountability (Hollin, 2001). The sentencing landscape changed to "get tough" laws, and community corrections followed suit by moving back to surveillance and punishment models.

The third pendulum swing happened in the 1990s in response to new research findings (McGuire, 1995). A new way of summarizing studies, a meta-analysis, gave researchers a better look at rehabilitation outcomes (Cullen and Gendreau, 2000). Unlike the old-style research review, in which individual studies were basically counted up as evidence for or against a theory, a meta-analysis takes into account evidence across all studies.[1] The new analyses showed what the 1970s studies had missed. When studies were lumped together, it may have appeared that nothing worked, but it became apparent from the meta-analysis that some approaches worked while other approaches clearly did not. Outcomes were mixed, depending on the approach. In fact, many treatments reduced recidivism, some by as much as 25 to 30 percent. Most punishment-oriented programs (e.g., boot camps, wilderness programs, electronic monitoring, home incarceration), however, were not effective, and some punishment-oriented programs that lacked a treatment component actually increased recidivism (Gendreau et al., 2002; Gendreau, Little, and Goggin, 1996; Gibbs, 1986; Taxman, 1999).

## Why Does Evidence-Based Practice Matter?

The new findings on effectiveness have challenged some older ideas of what people think should work. One well-publicized example is the rise and fall of correctional boot camps. Modeled after military-style boot camps, these punitive programs enjoyed a wide popularity in the 1980s and were heralded in numerous articles and press releases. Correctional boot camps were first opened for adults in 1983 and were subsequently applied to juveniles as well. The evidence for this approach was based on the belief that a disciplined military experience can change youth for the

---

[1] A baseball analogy is sometimes used to illustrate the difference between the two review styles. Older reviews that simply count studies are like keeping a score of the number of baseball games during a season where a batter hit or did not hit a ball. The meta-analytic format is more like a batting average, in that it takes into account how many times a batter hit a ball relative to the number of times up per game. Thus, it is a more sophisticated way to look at information because it takes into account the treatment impact across all studies.

better. Despite the enormous popularity of these "get tough" programs, the bulk of the research has shown that they have no effect on recidivism (Andrews et al., 1990; Gendreau et al., 2002; Gibbs, 1986; Taxman, 1999).

Boot camps are a good example of why intuitive beliefs can be hard to resist. Their instinctive appeal may lead to the investment of huge amounts of resources without much theory or research to back it up. Says one reviewer, "These ideas could certainly not have come out of the 25,000 or so studies published in the last 25 years in the learning and behavior modification literatures. . . . Even a casual reading of these literatures would clearly indicate that the 'get-tough' strategies . . . have no hope of reducing recidivism" (Gendreau et al., 2002). Without outcome research to indicate which programs have an impact, corrections professionals are stuck with their own intuition and "commonsense" beliefs. Few other fields would allow this. It would be unthinkable for modern doctors to discount research studies and instead rely on a commonsense approach to treating cancer, heart disease, or diabetes. In medicine, there is simply too much at stake for a doctor not to rely on current research evidence. Unfortunately, as a group of prominent criminologists notes, criminal justice is one of the few fields that still tolerates quackery and "what is done in corrections would be grounds for malpractice in medicine" (Latessa, Cullen, and Gendreau, 2002). Evidence-based practice allows agents to move beyond commonsense or "seat-of-the pants" approaches and to rely instead on empirically proven methods.

Corrections still retains some of the assumptions it inherited from the last swing of the pendulum toward punishment. Many agents were trained during the "get-tough '80s." Even those hired in the 1990s were coached and mentored by those who honed their skills in the punishment era. Because of their training, some agents have come to believe that confrontational tactics are necessary because they are the only language offenders understand. Some agents adopt an abrasive style so that offenders will know how serious their offending behavior is and to make it clear that they (the agents) cannot be taken advantage of. However, new literature that speaks directly to probation and parole officers urges agents to suspend the belief that confrontational approaches are necessary. An alternative is to take a "firm, fair, and consistent" stance where agents work to form a positive, collaborative relationship with offenders while holding them accountable for their actions (Clark, 2006).

## What Are the Principles of Effective Interventions?

Research points to three main principles of effective interventions:[2]

1. **Risk**—Directing programs toward higher risk offenders.
2. **Needs**—Targeting behaviors that reduce crime.
3. **Responsivity**—Being responsive to offender style.

---

[2] Treatment integrity is sometimes talked about as a fourth evidence-based principle. This means that, beyond the three principles discussed in this guide, programs should be of sufficient length, have appropriate content, and be delivered by adequately trained staff so that they can achieve their aims (Taxman and Bouffard, 2000).

These principles suggest what agents can do now to change the probability of future criminal behavior (Andrews et al., 1990; Cullen, 2002; National Institute of Corrections, 2003; Taxman, Shepardson, and Byrne, 2004).

## Risk

Supervision and treatment resources should be targeted at offenders who are at a higher risk of reoffending. High-risk offenders have a greater need for positive skills and thinking strategies and thus have more room to show improvement. It is also more cost effective to invest resources in this population because high-risk offenders are more likely to commit new crimes. When supervision resources are focused on lower risk offenders, they tend to produce little or no improvement (Cullen, 2002). Pouring resources into this group may even make things worse. Assigning low-risk offenders to greater external controls and elevated treatment interventions actually increases recidivism for some offenders (Cullen, 2002). Systems that target high-risk populations with intensive supervision, smaller caseloads, and focused interventions will reap a greater "bang for the buck."

## Criminogenic Needs

Interventions should target factors that predict crime and that can be changed. Some predictors of crime, such as history of criminal behavior, are "static," which means that they cannot be changed. Others, like self-control, are "dynamic," which means that they can be changed. Dynamic needs are promising targets for reducing crime and helping offenders make other positive changes. Research identifies six dynamic risk factors that have a direct link to criminal behavior and thus are ways to reduce future criminal behavior (Andrews and Bonta, 2003):[3]

1. Improved self-control.
2. Increased circle of caring.
3. Engagement in prosocial values.
4. Increased contact with prosocial "faces and places."
5. Substance abuse treatment.
6. Reconnection to primary/healthy relationships.

### *Improved Self-Control*

People with low self-control are more likely to commit crimes. Agents can help offenders improve self-control by encouraging natural talents and interests, talking about what things worked for them in the past, and identifying and role-playing difficult situations. New brain research helps explain why these strategies work (Lipchik et al., 2005). The regions of the brain that are activated when someone

---

[3] For the purposes of this guide, the authors chose to rephrase the six criminogenic needs in terms of the goal rather than the deficit. Hence, "low self-control" becomes "improved self-control" and "antisocial personality" becomes "increased circle of caring."

becomes fearful or angry override logical decisionmaking capacities. People seem to be wired to give either rational responses or upset responses, but not both at the same time. Correctional agents should not expect thoughtful decisions from angry, frustrated, or fearful persons. Instead, by listening and focusing on positive aspects of the offender's life, an agent can create an atmosphere that improves self-control and promotes rational decisionmaking.

### *Increased Circle of Caring*

People who hold antisocial attitudes are less concerned about how their actions affect others. However, most offenders do have a small circle of people who are important to them. It is not that most offenders are totally unconcerned about others, but that their circle of caring is too small. Although an offender may care deeply about family members or gang friends, the circle of caring does not extend outside this small group. One way to address this is through connecting the offender to other parts of the community through employment, faith communities, and other types of civic participation. Another method, the "helper principle," works to identify ways an offender can give to others, such as through volunteering or mentoring (Maruna and LeBel, 2003; Toch, 2000).

### *Engagement in Prosocial Values*

A small circle of caring affects personal values. An offender may disassociate himself from the larger community and instead take on the antisocial values of a small group. Programs for engaging prosocial values include those that focus on increasing empathy and concern for others. An offender may also have ideas about people who have been positive influences in the past. As discussed in the next chapter, the focus should be on modeling prosocial behaviors and drawing out the offender's own resources and strengths whenever possible.

### *Changing Peer Groups To Include Prosocial Faces and Places*

Peer groups affect behavior; thus, criminal friends increase the likelihood of further criminal behavior. Borrowing from alcohol and drug recovery programs, agents encourage offenders to change "playgrounds and playmates" and advise alcoholics to stay away from "wet faces and wet places." Many of the strategies for increasing the circle of caring and engaging prosocial values are also helpful for increasing contact with prosocial faces and places.

### *Substance Abuse Treatment*

The relationship between substance abuse and criminal behavior is complex. Offenders may commit crimes while under the influence or to support a drug habit, and many forms of substance use are themselves illegal. The good news is that mandated alcohol and drug treatment is effective for a large percentage of clients (Brecht, Anglin, and Jung-Chi, 1993; Miller and Flaherty, 2000). However, one factor that influences treatment success is the extent to which offenders are prepared by agents to enter a program. For instance, a brief motivational interview before an outpatient or inpatient program significantly improves treatment outcome (Bien, Miller, and Boroughs, 1993; Brown and Miller, 1993). Thus, an agent potentially has a large role in improving an offender's success in substance abuse treatment (Taxman, 1999).

### Reconnection to Primary/Healthy Relationships

Family history has a strong impact on criminal behavior. Family members may have had substance abuse problems, encouraged antisocial values, or modeled criminal behavior. Many offenders have had few positive role models. Ruptures in primary relationships also may have eliminated potential helpers from offenders' lives. Agents can help identify positive friends and family members and encourage offenders to reconnect with these positive influences. Though corrections has not often included families in the rehabilitation process, engaging family and friends who can act as positive influences in the process can have a number of benefits (see *www.familyjustice.org* for one example).

## Responsivity

General responsivity means being responsive to or targeting the known predictors of recidivism (i.e., the six criminogenic needs listed in the previous section). General responsivity suggests that agents use cognitive behavioral, social learning, and other evidence-based strategies to address dynamic criminogenic needs (Andrews and Bonta, 2003). Several large research studies have shown that approaches that use techniques such as modeling and practice of positive behaviors, providing resources and referrals, and giving feedback on performance tend to address these needs better. For optimal learning, positive feedback should outweigh negative feedback by a 4 to 1 ratio (Cullen, 2002). Most of the suggestions in this guide also fit into the category of general responsivity.

Specific responsivity means that interventions will be more effective if they are tailored to the needs of the individual (Taxman, Shepardson, and Byrne, 2004). The adage, "Different strokes for different folks," applies here. The following three questions can guide an agent in tailoring an interaction to the needs of a given offender:

- How ready is this person to change this behavior?
- Why might this person want to change this behavior?
- What kind of interaction will be most effective with this person?

### How Ready Is This Person To Change This Behavior?

One way to tailor interactions is to consider the offender's readiness for change at the intake or case planning stage. Offenders in the earlier stages of change (see chapter 2) do not yet see the behavior as a problem. Thus, agents may need to gear interactions and referrals to raise awareness and build motivation for change. In contrast, offenders who have progressed in their motivation may need help increasing their cognitive and behavioral skills to help translate desire into action. It is also important to understand that an offender may vary significantly in his motivational attitude, depending on the behavior to be modified. Thus, an offender may want help with job training while believing that his drug use is not a problem. This motivational profile may complicate interactions, but the basic principle remains that in the offender's mind, the two issues are separate. For this reason, chapter 5 suggests ways to meet offenders where they are in their thinking about different behaviors.

### Why Might This Person Want To Change This Behavior?

A second way to tailor interactions is to consider the person's interests and priorities. For instance, one offender might be motivated to seek drug treatment because of the effect of drugs on his family, another might be motivated because of the financial or health consequences, and yet another might be motivated because of legal pressure. Chapter 2 suggests some properties of change that are generally more attractive, such as beliefs about personal control, competence, and relatedness, but individuals may have their own ideas about what benefits are most attractive to them. Many times, simply listening to what an offender talks about first or most often can give a clue as to what he finds important. In other instances, a simple question like "If you decided to do this, how would that make things better for you?" can help determine what reasons this person might have for taking action.

### What Kind of Interaction Will Be Most Effective With This Person?

A final way to tailor interactions with offenders is to consider capabilities such as learning style and intelligence. Some individuals learn well from written material, whereas others need a more hands-on approach. Offenders with co-occurring disorders might benefit from visual aids, more frequent meetings, tangible rewards, or a reminder phone call.[4] Taxman, Shepardson, and Byrne's *Tools of the Trade: A Guide to Incorporating Science Into Practice* 2004; (available at *www.nicic.org/Library/020095*) offers a number of additional suggestions for matching services to offender responsivity. With a base of general responsivity, specific responsivity is a way to fine-tune meetings to the individual.

## How Does Motivational Interviewing Fit In With Evidence-Based Practice?

Evidence-based practice highlights the important role that agents have in offender outcome. In the past, rehabilitation was primarily the domain of mental health professionals, but EBP emphasizes that frontline staff, such as probation and parole officers, also have the opportunity to influence the change process. For example, officers conduct assessments, meet regularly with offenders, determine to which programs offenders are referred, and can speak with offenders in ways that motivate change. EBP elevates the officer's role from that of a mere observer and reporter of

---

[4] In treatment planning, it may also be important to take into account individual demographic factors such as gender, age, ethnicity, and history of trauma, although less information is available on exactly how to match interventions to clients based on these variables.

compliance to that of a professional—someone who has specialized skills to influence positive behavior change.

Much has been written about the first two principles of effective practice—risks and needs—but much less information is available about ways to access offender responsivity (National Institute of Corrections, 2003). Discussions of responsivity have focused mainly on matching programs to offender learning styles and intelligence. However, even if an agent does a good job matching an offender's learning style and intelligence to specific programs, the offender may not be ready to engage in these programs. Because the system requires participation from the start, agents need to be able to motivate offenders to take action. Motivational interviewing provides a basis for carrying out the principle of responsivity by suggesting a style of communication that makes it more likely that offenders will listen, will be engaged in the process, and will be more ready to make changes.

## KEY POINTS

- Build collaborative relationships that both motivate and hold offenders accountable for their actions.

- Target supervision and treatment resources to offenders who are at a higher risk of reoffending.

- Target factors that predict crime and that can be changed.

- Help improve the offender's self-control by encouraging natural talents and interests, talking about what worked for an offender in the past, and identifying and role-playing difficult situations.

- Enlarge the offender's connections to other parts of the community through employment, faith communities, and other types of civic participation.

- Encourage an offender to change "playgrounds and playmates"—that is, to stay away from criminal friends and criminal behaviors.

- Tailor interactions and interventions to offender characteristics such as motivation, learning style, and intelligence.

- MI is the foundation for working with offender responsivity. It suggests questions and statements that make it more likely that offenders will think, talk, and act in a positive direction.

# CHAPTER 2

# How and Why People Change

Chapter 1 talked about some principles of good correctional practice. This chapter talks about how and why people change and shows how correctional agents can use this knowledge to engage offenders in the change process.

## Old Assumptions About Motivation

Historically, motivation has been treated as a fixed personal characteristic. That is, an offender showed a certain amount of motivation and if that amount was too low—or until he was ready to change—the agent could do little to influence the offender's outcomes. Under this model, the supervising agent acted as an enforcer of a legal contract but not necessarily as an active participant in the change process. One agent describes his role as follows:

> The defendant receives supervision in lieu of jail. In our initial meeting, and throughout our work together, I tell the defendant what is expected of him and make it clear what the penalties will be should he fail to comply. We have regular meetings to verify that he is making progress on his conditions and I answer any questions he might have. If he breaks the law or shows poor progress on his conditions, I see to it that appropriate sanctions are assessed. Throughout the process, he is well aware of the behavior that might send him to jail, and if he ends up there, it's his own behavior that gets him there.

Reflected in this statement is an agent who believes he or she is essentially cut out of the change process, except as an observer. Further, agents often judged an offender's potential to change according to the following criteria:

- **Agreement with the agent's views.** It is better if an offender agrees with the official views of why he has become involved with the criminal justice system, including the arrest report and the court's/board's judgment. The agent also hopes the offender will recognize the "wrongness" of his offending behavior and express an early desire to reform.

- **Acceptance of a diagnosis.** It is better if the offender accepts a mental health diagnosis given to him by a formal assessment, such as "alcoholism," "major depression," or "problems with anger management."

## CHAPTER 2

- **Showing distress.** It is better if the offender regrets having to go through the legal process of arrest, detention, court/board appearance(s), and supervision. Distress is a sign that the offender is taking the process seriously.

Based on early indicators like these, agents sometimes decided who was likely to succeed while under supervision. Agents were willing to work with those who seemed ready to commit to a program of change, but tended to dismiss those who were uncooperative as destined to fail.

Even though many agents claim to have a kind of "radar" about forecasting future behavior, research shows that guesses about who will succeed under supervision based on the offender's initial presentation are rarely reliable. In general, assumptions like the ones above have only a small effect on eventual outcomes (Miller, 1985). The larger determinants of outcome are yet to come. Agents do not have to wait around for an offender to "get motivated." They have many ways to raise motivation, even if an offender seems very unmotivated to begin with.

### New Findings on Motivation

Although compliance is one marker of success, the larger goal of supervision involves more than just having offenders "do what they're told." Compliance does not equal change. Consider two offenders who agree to complete an anger management class: One agrees because he wants to avoid jail; the other agrees because he is concerned that his angry outbursts are affecting his marriage. Both offenders may be compliant, but the second is more likely to make changes that reduce the probability of future criminal behavior. Offenders make choices that affect the safety of their families and communities. Thus, it is important not only that they successfully complete supervision, but also that they make changes that will help them integrate into mainstream society after supervision.

Short-term compliance is, of course, one part of corrections. But the drawback of using punishment to gain compliance is that it may take the focus off long-term change. In fact, the threat of punishment mostly teaches people how to avoid being punished in the future (Skinner, 1953). Change can occur for external reasons, but it is often weak and short lived (Ryan and Deci, 2000). If the goal is to encourage long-term behavior change, agents need to be able to use techniques that access internal motivation for change, rather than those that rely solely on external pressure. Exhibit 2–1 illustrates some of the markers that help determine whether an interaction moves the offender toward change. Offenders who are more ready for change are thinking about, talking about, and exploring the possibility of change.

Motivation is a good predictor of outcome (DiClemente, Bellino, and Neavins, 1999), and its role in criminal justice is becoming increasingly emphasized in research and practice (Clark et al., 2006; Mann, Ginsburg, and Weekes, 2002). We know, for instance, that:

**Exhibit 2–1.** Short-Term Markers of Long-Term Change

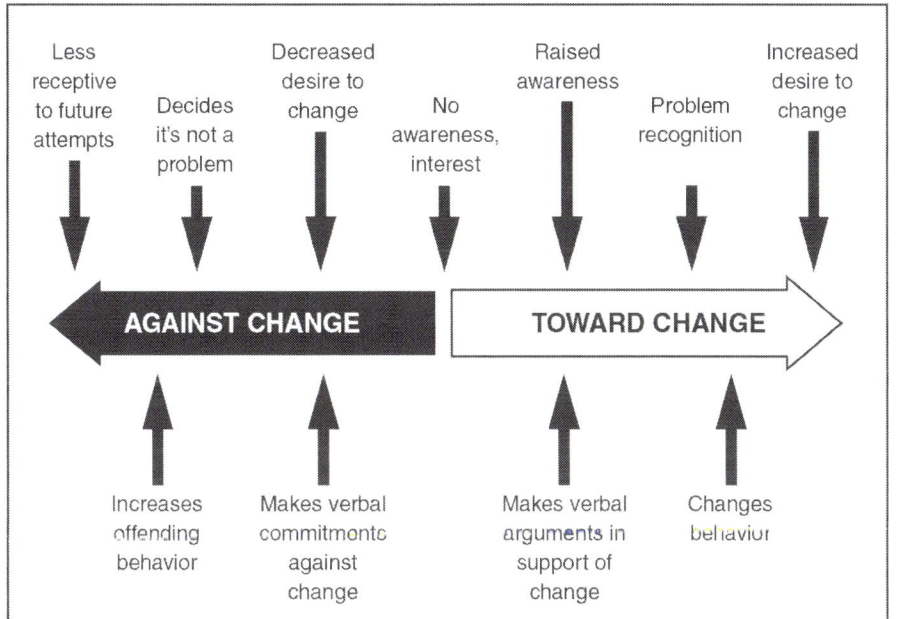

- **Motivation predicts action.** Motivation predicts how likely a person is to initiate and carry through with an action. Motivation is not a guarantee, but it does increase the likelihood of an action.

- **Motivation is behavior specific.** To talk about offenders as "unmotivated" in a global sense misses the point that people have different responses to different behaviors. For instance, an offender may be ready to attend marital counseling (because he thinks it would help his relationship) and pay fees (because it seems easy), but not be ready at all to attend a substance abuse evaluation (because he thinks he does not have a problem). Because people feel different about different behaviors, each behavior may need to be addressed separately.

- **Motivation is changeable.** Motivation is not a fixed trait like height or eye color; it can be increased or decreased. People frequently make changes after a significant event like a birth, marriage, or death of a loved one. Many young offenders simply mature out of criminal behavior. For others, even small events like a conversation with a friend or counselor can have an impact.

- **Motivation is interactive.** Talking with the agent can raise or lower the offender's motivation and guide what the offender talks and thinks about.

- **Motivation can be affected by both internal and external factors, but internally motivated change usually lasts longer.** Internal factors include how actions fit with personal values or goals ("How important is this change to me?") and beliefs about competence ("Am I going to be able to make this change?").

In corrections, internal and external forces work together to facilitate change. Because correctional agents work with a mandated population, change might begin because of external pressure (e.g., conditions of supervision), but later might be continued for internal reasons (e.g., the offender sees personal benefits). Agents can choose to emphasize short-term compliance as the primary goal, or they can choose to use strategies that help offenders make long-term progress.

## How People Change

The "Stages of Change" model, originally developed to explain how people quit smoking, is one way to think about behavior change (Prochaska, DiClemente, and Norcross, 1992; Prochaska and Levesque, 2002). According to this model, for most people, change is a process that unfolds over time. People can range from having no interest in making changes (precontemplation), to having some awareness or mixed feelings about change (contemplation), to preparing for change (preparation), to having recently begun to make changes (action), to maintaining changes over time (maintenance). Offenders in the earlier stages are less interested in change and may feel more coerced into acting, whereas offenders in the later stages are more interested in change for their own reasons. Exhibit 2–2 illustrates the stages of change, and exhibit 2–3 describes the stages in more detail.

In criminal justice, three major forces move people through the stages (Prochaska and Levesque, 2002). The first force is developmental. Criminality tends to decline with age. Most young people mature out of criminality, and so, to some extent, time is on the side of prosocial behavior change. The second force is environmental. Many times a personal event, such as the birth of a child, an illness, or a new friendship, will change a person's thinking about a behavior and motivate him or her to take action. The third force involves system efforts like legal sanctions, rehabilitation efforts, and interactions with agents. When considering the agent's role in the process, some principles of communication (which are discussed in chapters 3 and beyond) seem to work well throughout the process.

Exhibit 2–3 lists strategies that tend to be helpful at each of these three stages. The Stages of Change model can make interactions more efficient because it suggests

**Exhibit 2–2.** The Stages of Change

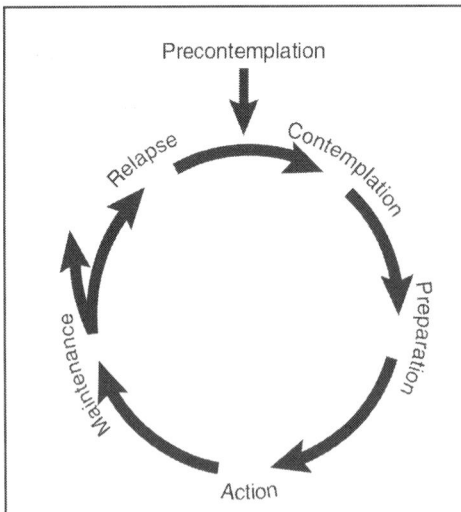

Source: Velasquez et al., 2001; adapted from Miller and Rollnick, 1991, 2002.

**Exhibit 2–3.** Issues and Strategies in the Stages of Change

| Stage | Issues | Strategies |
|---|---|---|
| Precontemplation | *"Nothing needs to change."*<br><br>Not considering change. Either avoids thinking about change or has decided that benefits of current behavior outweigh costs. May appear as denial or rationalization. | ■ Build rapport and trust.<br>■ Increase problem awareness; raise sense of importance of change. |
| Contemplation | *"I am considering change."*<br><br>Thinks there may be a problem, but has not decided what to do about it. May appear as ambivalence or mixed feelings. | ■ Acknowledge ambivalence (mixed feelings) about change.<br>■ Explore discrepancy between present behavior and personal values or goals.<br>■ Discuss pros and cons of change.<br>■ Talk about ways to "experiment" with change. |
| Preparation | *"I am figuring out how to change."*<br><br>Preparing to change by making small initial steps. Attitude may improve with a plan of action. May begin to ask questions about planning or how others have done it. | ■ Build confidence.<br>■ Talk about timing of change.<br>■ Present information, options, and advice.<br>■ Resist the urge to push; stay at the offender's pace. |
| Action | *"I'm working on reaching my goals."*<br><br>Actively making changes. May have found ways to manage urges or triggers that would lead back into problem behavior(s). | ■ Offer planning assistance.<br>■ Support and encourage efforts to change.<br>■ Develop reachable goals and monitor progress.<br>■ Help develop plans to maintain behavior over time. |
| Maintenance | *"I've made my changes. Now I have to keep it up."*<br><br>Maintaining changes over time. Developing ways to manage problems and stressors. Momentary slips are followed by remorse and renewed efforts. | ■ Support and encourage behavior change.<br>■ Talk about possible trouble spots and develop plans to manage relapse triggers. |
| Relapse | *"I've fallen back. Now all is lost."*<br><br>Has a slip and revisits the problem behavior. May appear as anger, demoralization, or denial of the behavior. Most reenter an earlier stage having learned something from the relapse. | ■ Address relapse, but do not add to feelings of shame.<br>■ Assess and discuss what went wrong.<br>■ Raise importance or confidence for another attempt. |

material to concentrate on and material to avoid. For instance, if a person is already making changes, the agent can lose ground by going over what has already been covered. On the other hand, if a person is not yet interested in change, the agent can waste time by giving advice and suggestions to someone who is not yet convinced that he needs or wants to change.

Looking at change in this way leads to four insights:

1. **Change tends to be a process.** Some people change quickly after a specific event (e.g., sudden insight, epiphany), but for most people, change is more complex. People may need to get information, weigh the pros and cons, and experiment with change before making a serious attempt to change.

2. **The stages suggest what kind of approach is most likely to help a person become more motivated.** When dealing with someone who is not ready to take action, the main goal may be to prepare that person for change. In the earlier stages, the goal is to raise the offender's awareness of the need for change. Someone in the middle stages of change may need help with planning or the timing of the change. In the later stages, suggestions and assistance with problem solving can be more helpful.

3. **Relapse is part of the cycle for many people.** In areas like dieting or quitting smoking or drinking, most people make several attempts before the change seems to stick. The same may be true for people under supervision. Change is a trial-and-error process for most people.

4. **Although the agent would like to see an offender move through all of the stages of change, a more practical goal during an individual reporting session may only be to raise motivation a little.** For instance, the goal of an early reporting session might be to inform the offender about the expectations of supervision and help him weigh the pros and cons of compliance, whereas the goal of a later session might be to encourage and assist in long-range planning.

## Why People Change

The Stages of Change model describes how people change, but it does not tell us why people change. We tend to assume that people weigh the pros and cons of their actions in a more or less rational manner before acting and that this pushes them through the stages. This logic was behind many of the "rational choice" approaches of the 1980s. If penalties were stiffer (e.g., longer jail terms, three-strikes laws), people would be less likely to commit crimes. Unfortunately, this logic does not always hold; people don't always consider the consequences before they act. For example, someone might decide that the immediate benefits of feeling good outweigh the future possibility of jail time.

A second idea that has been revised in recent years is the belief that in correctional settings, change must be externally imposed. After all, the logic goes, if an offender wanted to change on his own, he would have done it already. However, behavior change, even in corrections, arises from a mix of influences both from within the person (e.g., values, goals, sense of accomplishment) and from outside the person (e.g., threats, incentives, interpersonal pressure). In a study of clients entering alcohol treatment, 35 percent of court-mandated clients said that they did not feel they were being coerced into treatment; they felt they were doing it for their own reasons (Wild, Newton-Taylor, and Alletto, 1998). Conversely, among a group of self-referred clients, 37 percent felt that they were being coerced into treatment. These findings show that a considerable range of interests and goals exists even within groups of people who "have to" and people who "volunteer to" enter into treatment.

Why do some people make changes gladly, while others drag their feet and put in only the minimum amount of work? Self Determination Theory (SDT) gives us some insight into the conditions under which people make changes that stick over time (Deci and Ryan, 1985; Ginsburg et al., 2002; Markland et al., 2005; Ryan and Deci, 2000). SDT first assumes a motivational continuum (exhibit 2–4). As with the Stages of Change, people can range from having no interest in change to being very interested in change. People on the lower end of the continuum may have only external reasons for change, such as the threat of legal sanctions, whereas people on the upper end may also have internal reasons such as family, health, or a feeling of accomplishment.

**Exhibit 2–4.** Motivational Continuum

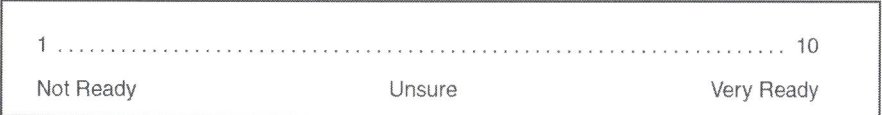

When people make changes for internal reasons, they try harder, are more satisfied, and stick with the changes longer than when they make changes for external reasons. In a treatment study that measured perceptions about internal and external motivation, the clients with the best outcomes were those who reported both a high degree of external pressure and significant internal reasons for wanting to succeed (Ryan, Plant, and O'Malley, 1995). Success was associated with both a high degree of internal motivation and a high degree of legal pressure, but externally motivated subjects had positive long-term outcomes only when they also had high levels of internal motivation. This suggests that people's perceptions about what is driving the change play a big part in the outcome. All changes are not created equally; the more a person owns the reasons for change, the more likely he or she is to succeed.

Of course, external coercion is a part of the criminal justice system. Studies have shown, however, that a person's perception of what is prompting the change is more important than what is actually prompting the change. According to SDT, agents can increase internal motivation for change by addressing three basic factors: autonomy, competence, and relatedness.

- **Autonomy.** Autonomy is an individual's perception of himself or herself as the determining agent of an action ("I chose to do this"). When people think that they are making changes for their own reasons, they work harder and are more likely to stick with the new behaviors. In fact, too much coercion can undermine internal motivation because it makes people feel they are being manipulated, which in turn makes them less likely to change (Deci and Ryan, 1985). Agents can help offenders build autonomy by acknowledging reluctance, providing options, and emphasizing personal choice. The agent may not be able to negotiate whether or not an offender complies with the supervision conditions, but he or she can frequently negotiate how and when the offender complies. This makes the offender feel that the decision to comply is under his control.

- **Competence.** Competence involves beliefs about confidence ("I can do this"). To change, a person needs to believe that change is both important and possible. Consider an offender who has been stealing to support his family. Even if the offender wants to change his behavior, he might have doubts about whether he would be able to hold a job or support his family on a lesser income. Many offenders come from backgrounds where expectations are low and examples of prosocial behavior are hard to find. Helping the offender set realistic goals, talking about personal strengths, and giving positive feedback on small successes (rather than focusing only on what the offender has not accomplished) can increase his sense of competence. In fact, encouragement from the agent may be the only positive feedback some offenders receive.

- **Relatedness.** Change is more likely when people are available to support the offender. This condition of relatedness gives a powerful explanation of why people sometimes act against their own self-interest (Deci and Ryan, 1985). For better or worse, people tend to behave like those with whom they associate. For instance, a youth offender might violate a curfew or rob a liquor store because it fits with the values of his peer group. Conversely, someone else might work two jobs, save money, or give up drinking because it is meaningful to his mother. These individuals engage in these behaviors because they are meaningful to others to whom they feel connected.

Relatedness also includes the relationship between an agent and offender. Agents can clarify their roles, model prosocial behavior, and help offenders develop problem-solving skills. A good working relationship will make interactions more efficient and effective (Ward and Brown, 2004). Meta-analyses show that the provider-client relationship plays a large role in client outcome (Hubble, Duncan, and Miller, 1999; Wampold et al., 1997). A critical finding drawn from more than 1,000 research studies concludes: "Putting this all into perspective, the amount of change attributable to the relationship is about seven times that of the amount attributable to a specific model or technique" (Hubble, Duncan, and Miller, 1999).

Although SDT does not totally explain why people change behavior, it provides certain clues as to when change is more likely to occur. Offenders who have internal reasons to change, who feel confident about the new behaviors, and who have others to support and encourage them are more likely to make positive, lasting changes. Conversely, offenders who feel coerced, manipulated, or unsupported may make superficial changes, but more often than not, their old behaviors reappear quickly after the external contingencies are removed.

## KEY POINTS

- Motivation predicts behavior and is changeable. An agent can do a lot to increase (or decrease) an offender's motivation to change.

- Both internal and external factors can affect motivation, but internally motivated change usually lasts longer.

- The Stages of Change model describes the process people go through in thinking about change.

- People change when a new action or behavior is more in line with their personal beliefs or values. Each person is motivated to change by unique factors.

- Agents can support an offender's internal motivation to change by highlighting autonomy, competence, and relatedness.

# CHAPTER 3

# The Motivational Interviewing Style

Motivational interviewing (MI) is a way of talking with offenders to build their internal motivation for change. MI suggests ways to use questions and statements strategically to make it more likely offenders will talk in a positive direction. This chapter covers the logic behind the MI approach, including its basic principles, assumptions, and thoughts about how MI facilitates change.

## What Is Motivational Interviewing?

MI arose during the 1980s from alcohol counseling research. This research began to suggest that certain types of brief counseling interactions could be as effective as more lengthy interventions and that a certain kind of provider style was better at eliciting change. Two recent reviews of more than 70 MI outcome studies in different areas strongly support the effectiveness of the MI approach (Hettema, Steele, and Miller, 2005; Rubak et al., 2005). MI performed significantly better than other approaches in three out of four published research studies, and outperformed traditional advice-giving 80 percent of the time. Even when looking at single encounters of 15 minutes or less, 64 percent of studies showed a lasting effect using this method.

MI is a person-centered method of fostering change by helping a person explore and resolve ambivalence (Miller and Rollnick, 2002). Rather than using external pressure, MI looks for ways to access internal motivation for change. It borrows from client-centered counseling in its emphasis on empathy, optimism, and respect for client choice (Rogers, 1961). MI also draws from self-perception theory, which says that a person becomes more or less committed to an action based on the verbal stance he or she takes (Bem, 1972). Thus, an offender who talks about the benefits of change is more likely to make that change, whereas an offender who argues and defends the status quo is more likely to continue his present behavior. Finally, MI is logically connected to the Stages of Change model discussed in chapter 2 (Prochaska, DiClemente, and Norcross, 1992). For most people, ambivalence—mixed feelings, hesitancy, arguments against change—is a normal part of the change process. Most offenders will have mixed feelings about quitting drugs, finding a job, participating in treatment, and attending supervision meetings. Although MI appears to work throughout the change process, it is particularly suited to individuals who are resistant, reluctant, or in an early stage of their thinking about change.[1]

Although MI suggests some tangible strategies, it is better thought of as a style of interaction that follows these basic principles:

- **Express empathy.** Empathy is about good rapport and a positive working environment. It is an attempt to understand the offender's mindset, even though the agent may not agree with the offender's point of view. Empathy also involves an effort to draw out concerns and reasons for change from the offender, instead of relying on the agent's (or court's/board's) agenda as the sole persuasion strategy.

- **Roll with resistance.** It is normal to have mixed feelings when thinking about change. Therefore, the agent does not argue with the offender. As one writer put it, "Do not argue or debate with the client. You are not likely to change her mind through reasoning. If this approach was going to work, it would have worked by now" (Berg, 1994). Rolling with resistance means finding other ways to respond when the offender challenges the need for change.

- **Develop discrepancy.** Discrepancy is the feeling that one's current behavior is out of line with one's goals or values. Rather than telling the offender why he should change, the agent asks questions and makes statements to help the offender identify his own reasons for change.

- **Support self-efficacy.** A person is more likely to follow through with behavior he believes he has freely chosen and believes he can accomplish. Therefore, the agent remains optimistic, reminds the offender of personal strengths and past successes, and affirms all efforts toward change.

In emphasizing respect, optimism, and choice, MI clearly differs from confrontational approaches. It also differs somewhat from the helper approaches that are more prevalent in social work and counseling. MI emphasizes listening while looking for ways to guide the interaction toward positive talk.

Initially, some agents might view MI as a slow and passive process, especially as compared with the drama of direct confrontation. Some agents may worry that a quieter approach may signal to the offender that his reluctance to change his behavior is acceptable. However, the outcomes of more than 70 studies show that this is not the case. Aggressive confrontation usually pushes offenders backward in the change process.

---

[1] Because they are often talked about together, MI is sometimes confused with the Stages of Change model. However, the two are not necessarily connected. Stages of Change is a theory of behavior change. MI is an intervention strategy for building motivation for change.

In the MI model, agents interact with offenders to produce positive change. Because people are more likely to make changes that they believe are personally important and that they have talked about (see exhibit 3–1), agents use questions and reflections strategically to elicit positive talk from the offender (Kear-Colwell and Pollock, 1997; Moyers, Miller, and Hendrickson, 2005).

**Exhibit 3–1.** Probability of Behavior Change

| Statement | Probability of Behavior Change |
|---|---|
| Officer talks about why change is important. Probationer nods head. | (low) |
| Probationer thinks about why change is personally important. | (moderate) |
| Probationer talks about why change is personally important. | (higher) |
| Probationer makes verbal commitment to change. | (high) |

## What Are the Basic Assumptions of Motivational Interviewing?

An agent's view of the nature of offenders can determine whether he or she will be able to embrace the MI style. There are three basic views of human morality. One view is that all people are basically good and will commit harmful acts only if they cannot achieve their goals through acceptable means. A second view is that most offenders are born bad and that antisocial acts are part of their basic nature. This view can lead to aggressive confrontation, a failure to recognize an offender's positive efforts, and negative interpretations of otherwise normal behavior. A third, balanced view assumes that offenders, like other people, are equally capable of good and bad actions and that both sides are already present in each person (Ward and Brown, 2004). Thus, working with offenders is more like "drawing out" preferred behaviors than "putting in" something offenders lack. MI assumes that all offenders are entitled to be treated with respect because of their essential worth as human beings. This is consistent with a strengths-based perspective, which holds that offenders already possess a range of talents, abilities, skills, and resources (Rapp,

1998; Saleebey, 1992). The goal is to draw out these positive resources to help people exit the criminal justice system and improve their lives. Agents can detest the illegal behaviors but at the same time believe that every person is worthy of their best efforts.

## How Does Motivational Interviewing Facilitate Change?

Given its excellent track record, interest in how MI works has increased. Research suggests that MI facilitates change by promoting three conditions (Amrhein et al., 2003; Moyers and Martin, 2006; Moyers, Miller, and Hendrickson, 2005):

- It reduces resistance.
- It raises discrepancy.
- It elicits change talk.

### It Reduces Resistance

Because they view motivation as a fixed offender trait, some agents feel the best strategy is to confront denial, rationalization, and excuses directly:

- You've got a problem.
- You have to change.
- If you violate, you'll go back to jail. Is that what you want?

Other officers shy away from a heavy-handed approach, relying instead on suggestions or logical persuasion.

- Can't you see how this behavior is affecting your kids?
- Why don't you just . . . ?
- Here's how you should go about this.

Unfortunately, the evidence suggests that both of these strategies tend to make things worse, especially early on in the interaction. When confronted with external pressure, the typical response is to defend the status quo. The agent confronts and the offender resists, as shown in exhibit 3–2.

**Exhibit 3–2.** Agent Confrontation and Offender Resistance

| Agent Confronts | Offender Resists |
| --- | --- |
| You've got a problem because . . . | No, I don't because . . . |
| Why don't you . . . | That won't work for me because . . . |
| If you don't you'll . . . | My friend did and he . . . |

Agents can and should enforce the appropriate sanctions, but confrontation between the offender and his own issues (discrepancy) is more conducive to long-term change than confrontation between the offender and the agent (coercion). An alternative to confronting resistance directly is to reflect what the offender has said and emphasize personal responsibility. The section "Reflect What You Are Hearing or Seeing" in chapter 4 provides a number of examples of ways to respond to resistance.

## It Raises Discrepancy

Some probationers enter supervision in the precontemplation stage, not thinking that they have any reason to change. Others enter supervision in the preparation or action stage, having already acknowledged the problem and needing minimal assistance to begin to change. Throughout supervision, mixed feelings are a normal part of the change process. (See "How People Change" in chapter 2.)

Officers have long been taught to see ambivalence as a classic form of denial, yet to the motivationally inclined officer, it demonstrates a reason for optimism. Rather than being a sign that a person is moving away from change, ambivalence signals that change may be on the horizon. The person is thinking about change. Ambivalence makes change possible; it is a precursor to positive behavior change.

The best interaction is one in which the probationer voices the arguments for change. First, the officer works to establish a positive and collaborative relationship with the probationer. A positive relationship creates a place in which probationers can feel comfortable talking about change. Second, the officer identifies and calls attention to the probationer's ambivalence about change. The gap between the probationer's goals or values and his current behavior creates discrepancy. This gap becomes the ground for amplifying the probationer's own reasons for change.

Everyone is motivated for something, but movement from harmful behaviors to more healthy behaviors requires the resolution of ambivalence. The balance tips to one side or the other. A small percentage of probationers have no ambivalence about their current behavior. However, the large majority of probationers will enter the supervision system with some concerns about their behavior (if only about the legal consequences). Where this discrepancy leads depends on whether an officer recognizes the discrepancy and uses it to elicit talk that leads to change.

## It Elicits Change Talk

People can literally talk themselves in and out of change; hence, agents can learn to recognize the kind of talk that leads to change. The agent's speech sets the tone for the offender's speech, which, in turn, influences the ultimate outcome. An offender may come in with a certain range of readiness for change, but what the agent says makes a difference in where the offender ends up on the motivational continuum, as illustrated in exhibit 3–3.

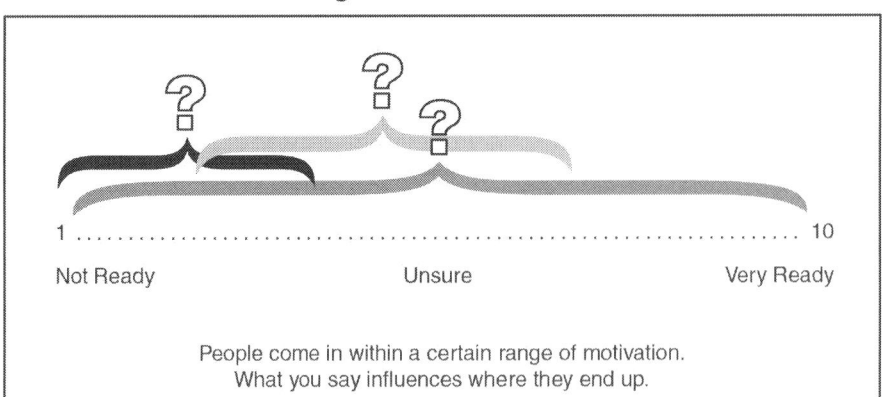

**Exhibit 3–3.** Movement Along the Motivational Continuum

1 .................................................................. 10
Not Ready                  Unsure                      Very Ready

People come in within a certain range of motivation.
What you say influences where they end up.

Linguists have studied the speech content of motivational interviews—the actual words spoken between an agent and a client—looking for clues to predict behavior change (Amrhein et al., 2003). They divided motivational speech into five categories: desire, ability, reasons, need, and commitment language (sometimes referred to by the acronym DARN–C).

- **Desire.** Desire expresses a wish to attain or succeed:
  "I wish I could get off supervision." "I really want to get a job."

- **Ability.** Ability talks about confidence:
  "I could quit smoking pot." "I believe I could get back with my spouse. I've done it before, and it's possible."

- **Reasons.** Reasons involve a tangible incentive, motive, or rationale for change. For instance, reasons might focus on how change would make things better or how continued behavior would make things worse:
  "At least my wife would quit bugging me if I found a job." "Smoking crack really flares up my asthma."

- **Need.** Need, at least initially, may overlap with reasons. After a while, need may involve more emotion: "I've got to. I must." Need moves beyond logical reasons into urgency. Where reason says, "I should," need says, "I must."

- **Commitment.** Commitment expresses a readiness or agreement to change:
  "Five job applications? Yeah, I'll do that."

Within this model, it was not so much the frequency of the speech, but rather the quality and strength of the language that predicted who was and was not successful. The first four kinds of speech (i.e., "DARN") moved people toward change, but commitment speech sealed the deal. Exhibit 3–4 shows the flow of talk that best predicts later change. Speech about desire, ability, reasons, and need lead to commitment talk, which leads to change in behavior. "I'll try" is a weak statement as compared to "I will," which conveys much more strength of commitment. A wise trade would exchange five "I'll try"s for one "I will."

**Exhibit 3–4.** Flow of Change Talk

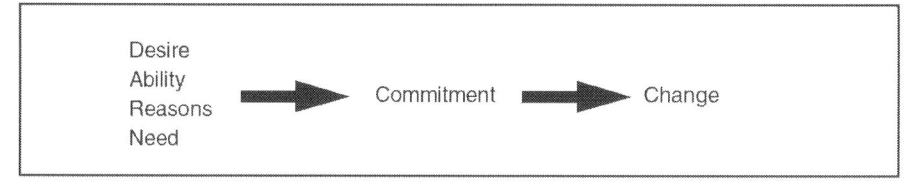

```
Desire
Ability
Reasons      ──▶   Commitment   ──▶   Change
Need
```

Although chapters 5 and 6 talk more directly about ways to draw out the kind of talk that leads to change, this chapter has hinted at three principles:

1. **Because offender speech is a predictor of outcome, agents should encourage offenders to talk about why and how they might change.** Ideally, the agent should talk only as much as is necessary to keep the offender talking in a positive direction. Offender speech is a good predictor of later change.

2. **Agents should avoid arguing with offenders.** Aggressive persuasion and confrontation tend to make a person more resistant, thereby decreasing DARN–C talk. If confronted in a heavy-handed style, an offender is more likely to argue with the agent and defend his current behavior.

3. **Agents should ask questions that elicit the kind of talk they want to hear.** The offender speaks about his interests and motivation, and the agent keeps track of what might motivate this person in order to direct the conversation better.

## For Whom Is Motivational Interviewing Best Suited?

MI is an evidence-based practice: that is, good evidence exists that MI works well as the preferred style for talking about change. However, less information is available about who is more or less likely to benefit from MI. The approach has a good track record in studies with schizophrenic, depressed, and antisocial clients and others with relatively low cognitive functioning (Hettema, Steele, and Miller, 2005; Project MATCH Research Group, 1998; Rubak et al., 2005). Recent findings from large alcohol and drug treatment studies suggest that MI may work particularly well with people who are early in the change process and those who are angrier or more resistant to change (Project MATCH Research Group, 1997, 1998). It may seem obvious that for people in the early stages of change, the goal is to increase motivation. For those in the later stages of change, the goal is not to motivate, but to encourage and support continued efforts. The finding about resistance may make less intuitive sense. However, research has shown clearly that the more resistant the client, the better MI seems to work as compared with other approaches.

The available research on the use of MI both in criminal justice settings and in other contexts suggests that MI can work for a wide range of offenders. MI has been shown to be useful for increasing motivation for some observable behaviors, such as paying fees, finding a job, or engaging in alcohol or drug treatment (Ginsburg et al., 2002; Harper and Hardy, 2000; Vivian-Byrne, 2004), MI also has an excellent track record in preparing people to engage in alcohol and drug treatment programs (Baker et al., 2002; Daley et al, 1998; Miller, Meyers, and Tonigan, 1999). It also has been well validated with adolescent substance abusers (Dunn et al., 2004; Erickson, Gerstle, and Feldstein, 2005; Monti et al., 1999; Monti, Colby, and O'Leary, 2001; Tevyaw and Monti, 2004). Although there are published accounts of the use of MI with sex offenders and other character-disordered persons (Berk, Berk, and Castle, 2004; Easton, Swan, and Sinha, 2000; Mann and Rollnick, 1996; Marques et al., 1999), less information is available about whether or how MI might need to be modified for use with these populations.

Because MI relies on cognition and communication, the interviewee must be reasonably verbal and capable of abstract thinking for this approach to work effectively. Using MI with persons with co-occurring mental illness or more limited cognitive functioning may require modifications to the basic MI skill set, such as simplifying questions, refining reflective listening skills, heightening affirmations, and integrating psychiatric issues into discussions (Martino et al., 2000, 2002). Taxman, Shepardson, and Byrne's *Tools of the Trade: A Guide to Incorporating Science Into Practice* (2004; available at *www.nicic.org/Library/020095*) provides other examples of issues that might be relevant to different offender types.

## KEY POINTS

- MI is a client-centered, directive approach that emphasizes listening and looking for ways to direct the interaction toward positive talk.

- Mixed feelings, hesitancy, and even arguments against change are a normal part of the change process.

- Aggressive confrontation pushes offenders backward in the change process.

- MI facilitates change by reducing levels of resistance, raising discrepancy, and increasing positive change talk.

- The best interaction is one in which the offender gives the reasons for change.

- Identifying and calling attention to an offender's ambivalence can help him determine whether his behavior is in conflict with other personal values.

- Talk about desire, ability, reasons, and need leads to commitment talk, which, in turn, predicts behavior change.

# CHAPTER 4

# Preparing for Change

The old adage, "You can't make a person change if they don't want to," is only partially true. In fact, agents may be able to do a lot to prepare an offender to find a job, address chaotic family life, or give up substance abuse. The art lies in getting the person to want to make changes in these areas. Frequently, agents want to jump straight to problem solving. However, this ignores the fact that most people need to be prepared for change. For this reason, this chapter outlines basic strategies to prepare a person to think about change.

Four main techniques (sometimes referred to as "OARS," for open-ended questions, affirm, reflect, and summarize) help agents guide the conversation toward change. These techniques are a gas pedal for the conversation. Chapter 6 talks about ways to use these techniques strategically to steer conversations, but steering in itself is worthless unless the car is in gear and moving forward.

## Ask Open-Ended Questions

Closed questions ask for yes or no responses; open-ended questions ask for longer answers or elaboration. Both kinds of questions may be useful during an interview, depending on the purpose of the question. For instance, agents may ask closed questions to gather information or document compliance:

- Have you had any contact with the victim?
- Are you making a payment today?
- Has there been any change in your residence?

Because the interactions between agents and offenders are often brief, the agent may need to move through some aspects of the interview quickly. However, if the purpose of the question is to gather detailed information or to encourage the offender to think about the answer, open-ended questions are usually better. Exhibit 4-1 illustrates the difference between the two types of questions.

Closed questions are less good at pulling out more detailed information because they merely confirm or disconfirm the interviewer's opinion. They tell the agent whether his or her guess was right or wrong, but they do not get the offender talking

CHAPTER 4

**Exhibit 4–1.** Closed Versus Open-Ended Questions

| Closed Question | Open-Ended Question |
| --- | --- |
| Do you feel you have a problem with alcohol? | What problems has your alcohol use caused for you? |
| Is it important to you to complete supervision successfully? | How important is it for you to complete supervision successfully? |
| Anything else? | What else? |

or thinking about the answer. In contrast, open-ended questions ask for a longer, more considered response.

Consider the difference between two basic questions: "Anything else?" and "What else?" Changing a single word dramatically increases the quality of the response. The first question calls for a simple yes or no. If the question is intended to encourage the person to talk, it falls flat. In contrast, the second question sets the stage for a more detailed and thoughtful answer.

One place for open-ended questions is in the assessment portion of an interview. The following dialogue illustrates the use of open-ended questions to gather information about job history.

> **Agent:** Tell me a little about your job history. *[Open-ended question.]*
>
> **Offender:** I'm a certified pipe welder, mostly commercial stuff.
>
> **A:** How long have you been doing that? *[Closed question.]*
>
> **O:** I guess about 5 years.
>
> **A:** What other skills do you have? *[Open-ended question.]*
>
> **O:** Sometimes they call me out to operate some of the heavy equipment when people are out.
>
> **A:** So that might be a possibility again at some point. What other things have you done? *[Open-ended question.]*
>
> **O:** Well, I was a checker at a supermarket when I was younger, but you can't really support a family on that.
>
> **A:** OK, so you might be able to do supermarket work as a last resort, but it doesn't really look like a long-term solution. What are some of the things you think might get in the way of you finding the kind of job you want? *[Reflection; open-ended question.]*

**O:** Well, I'd probably have to pass a drug screen.

**A:** So if you weren't using, that would make things easier for you. What other things would you need to do to make yourself more marketable? *[Reflection; open-ended question.]*

In addition to gathering some basic information about vocational skills, the agent inserts a key question ("What things might get in the way?") to gather information and get the offender thinking about potential solutions. Open-ended questions such as the following keep a person talking—they pull out speech:

- Tell me about your drug use.
- What's that like for you?
- What was your life like before you started drinking?
- How do you want things to end up when you're done with supervision? Where do you want to be?
- What other ideas do you have? What else might work for you?

Another advantage of open-ended questions is that they encourage a person to think about what he or she is saying. The following interaction shows an agent using closed questions to try to motivate an offender to seek drug treatment. The agent uses questions to try to raise awareness of and interest in change, but phrases them in such a way that the offender instead becomes defensive. Closed questions are unlikely to produce the kind of talk the agent is looking for.

**Agent:** You don't think your drug use is a problem?

**Offender:** Not really. When I used to use, I would just do it every once in a while, and I can't see how it really hurt anything.

**A:** How about your kids? Don't you think that your drug use has a negative impact on them?

**O:** No, because they didn't see me use.

**A:** Even if you don't use in front of them, aren't you afraid that it might put them at risk? I mean, how can you care for your kids if you're high?

**O:** It doesn't really affect them. Because when I used to use a neighbor always took care of them. She just kept them overnight.

This dialogue stalls because the offender feels that the agent is using questions to trick him into entering drug treatment. He counters each question with an excuse to avoid being logically ambushed by the agent. He is thinking more about how to counter the agent's point and less about what his responses actually mean.

# CHAPTER 4

Open-ended questions, on the other hand, are usually better for increasing motivation—especially internal motivation—to change. Here are some examples:

- What concerns do you (does your wife, girlfriend, etc.) have about your drinking?
- How has this caused trouble for you?
- What do you think might happen if you got another positive urinalysis?
- If you did go ahead and finish the class, how would that make things better for you?

Questions like these encourage the offender to think about how his present behavior creates difficulties for him and how things would look if he changed that behavior. They help shift the balance toward action. Open-ended questions can also help a person arrive at a specific plan of action:

- There are a few things that might work for you (provide a short list). Which of these would you like to try?
- What would you like to work on first?
- Who would (or will) help you to . . . ?
- What worked for you in the past?

None of these questions is a magic bullet—a person can always shut down or refuse to answer—but they increase the probability that a person will speak and think more productively. The following example illustrates how the previous dialogue regarding drug treatment might have been different if the agent had used open-ended questions to target the offender's interest in change:

**Agent:** What effect do you think your drug use has on your kids? *[Open-ended question.]*

**Offender:** I don't really think it affects them. They're never around when I'm using.

**A:** You're careful to make sure that it doesn't affect them. *[Reflection, affirmation.]*

**O:** Well yeah, I don't want them to have to deal with what I went through as a kid.

**A:** What was that like? *[Open-ended question.]*

**O:** I had a bad time of it, with no father and a drug-using mother.

**A:** . . . and you want something better for your kids. *[Reflection.]*

**O:** Absolutely. That's no way to be raised.

**A:** What are you afraid might happen to the kids? I mean, what things are you worried about? *[Open-ended question.]*

**O:** When Joe comes over, there's always pressure to use. Even if I don't take a hit, he might. He doesn't care whether the kids are there or not, and I think it could get ugly.

**A:** How so? *[Open-ended question.]*

**O:** He gets mean and loud and somebody usually ends up calling the cops.

**A:** You want to make sure your kids have a better time of it than you did, and you're afraid that situations like that might place them at risk. *[Reflection.]*

The agent uses open-ended questions to help the offender think about the effects of his drug use on his children. Although the offender has not yet agreed to enter drug treatment, this conversation has been productive. The offender has provided information about what is important to him (having a safe environment for his children to grow up in), a situation he thinks is particularly risky (when Joe comes over), and more general thoughts about change (how being around drug-using friends affects his children). From here, the agent might ask about the possible benefits of entering treatment or perhaps even leave the topic for the next visit. Either way, the offender leaves the appointment with something to think about.

Unlike the agent in the first dialogue, this agent does not use heavy-handed persuasion. The offender clearly has mixed feelings about his drug use, and the agent uses questions and statements to pull out these thoughts. Also notice that the offender is doing most of the talking—another indicator of a successful interaction. Finally, the tone of the conversation leaves the door open to future conversations. In contrast to the first dialogue, the offender probably feels that the agent is looking out for his best interest and the best interests of his children.

## Affirm Positive Talk and Behavior

The classic book on business management *How to Win Friends and Influence People* talks about Andrew Carnegie's reasons for picking Charles Schwab as the first president of U.S. Steel. Schwab had a remarkable way of getting things done that made him well worth his million-dollar-a-year salary. At the heart of Schwab's genius was his ability to motivate through encouragement. Schwab said, "I am anxious to praise.... If I like anything, I am hearty in my approbation and lavish in my praise" (Carnegie, 1998). Schwab went out of his way to recognize positive efforts.

Unfortunately, many people do just the opposite—they criticize what bothers them and stay quiet when they see something they like. Some probation and parole officers avoid praise because they believe that offenders should not be rewarded for doing what they are ordered to do. Others are reluctant to tell an offender that he is doing well because of the chance that the offender has been lying all along. The best approach for an agent who wants to avoid being wrong is to stick with the "tough as nails" approach. However, if an agent believes that his or her role involves helping the offender change his behavior, then incentives, and especially verbal recognition, must be part of the equation. Positive statements build rapport, provide feedback, and make positive behaviors more likely (Farbring, 2002).

One kind of affirmation reinforces something the person has done or intended to do:

- Thanks for coming in on time. It helps me to keep things on track.
- You're doing nice work on your community service requirement.
- Thanks for telling me about that.
- It's clear that you have thought a lot about this.
- It seems like that will really work for you.

Another kind of affirmation calls attention to something admirable or interesting about the person:

- You care a lot about your kids and want to make sure they're safe.
- Your willingness to respond to the hard questions shows that you're really thinking about this.
- You're the kind of person who speaks up when something bothers you, and that's a real strength.
- You have a lot of leadership qualities. It's clear that people listen to you.

Some psychologists have suggested that the optimal ratio for positive behavior change is about four affirmations for every critical comment (Cullen, 2002). A less rigid rule of thumb is to use as many affirmations as possible and affirm any behavior that you want to see again. Some agents look for ways to praise things that an offender has done or intended to do, while others take time to learn about an offender's family, hobbies, and strengths so that they can show a genuine interest in his personal life.

Another affirmation strategy is to "blame" people for their successes (Clark, 1998). Rather than dwelling on failures, this involves paying special attention to personal successes. A few "how" questions can reinforce positive efforts and build confidence:

- How did you do this?
- How did you know that would work?
- You know, a lot of people under supervision never seem to get it together, but you have really found a way to make this happen. You found a job in spite of the difficulties with childcare, and are even ahead on your fees. How did you manage to do all that?

Agents may also tie affirmations to other incentives. For instance, the system may provide incentives for offenders who complete tasks on time, find jobs, pay fees, or stay out of trouble. Each time agents provide an incentive for good behavior, they increase the probability that the offender will behave that way again. Because of this, agents (and systems) should develop specific incentives for positive behavior and look for ways to reward people who are doing well. A list of incentives might include the following:

- Verbal affirmations.
- Community service credit for a general equivalency diploma (GED) or treatment.
- Travel permits.
- Fax or mail-in reporting.
- A more flexible reporting schedule, such as late-night/early-morning or front-desk reporting.
- Counting class attendance as an office visit.
- Decreasing meeting or urinalysis frequency.
- Certificates of completion or reference letters.
- Extended time to complete specific requirements.
- Early termination of supervision.

The following examples show agents commending offenders for meeting supervision conditions and suggesting ways of relaxing those conditions as appropriate:

- **Person arrives on time:**
  Thanks for showing up on time. I know it's hard for you to get here this early, and it shows that you're sticking with this.

- **Clean urinalysis (UA):**
  You have another negative UA, so I think we can go back to monthly UAs. You are doing really good work staying clean and I'm making sure to document that in my case notes. Obviously you're working hard at this, and I'm wondering what you've been doing to make sure that you stay clean. How is this different than last time?

- **Prompt payment of fees:**
  Payment? Good, I think that brings you almost up to what you owe. You always make some kind of payment, and I think that's really helping you out. In fact, you're doing well enough that it might be possible to submit a petition to reduce your community service requirement for on-time payment of fees. Is that something you'd like to look into?

## Reflect What You Are Hearing or Seeing

New agents often underestimate the power of an aptly placed statement. Reflections disarm; reflections affirm; reflections guide. For these reasons, reflections are frequently a core part of counseling, negotiation, and sales techniques. For instance, in William Ury's book on business negotiation, the chief task in the opening minutes of a negotiation is to reflect and summarize what the other person is saying: "It is not enough for you to listen to the other side. They need to know that you have heard what they have said. So reflect back what you hear" (Ury, 1993). Likewise, in his bestselling book on crisis negotiation, Frederick Lanceley writes, "The negotiator works with the subject's feelings, values, lifestyles and opinions to resolve the incident. . . . It is far more effective for the negotiator to demonstrate understanding through active listening" (Lanceley, 2003).

At their core, reflections are guesses as to what an offender is saying or thinking. Reflections do not indicate agreement with the offender; rather, they tell the offender that the agent has been listening and help the offender hear what he has been saying. They may repeat or rephrase what an offender has said, summarize an emotion, or point out mixed feelings. More advanced reflections may direct the conversation by emphasizing part of what an offender has said or pointing out a connection between two statements (see chapter 5).

Two basic principles help raise the quality of reflections:

1. **Strip the statement down.** State only the most important elements of what the person has said. Avoid starting reflections with stems like, "So, what I'm hearing you say is that . . . ." or "What you're telling me is that . . . ." If the offender sounds angry, say, "It makes you angry," or simply, "You're angry." In fact, the best reflections may only be a word or two.

    o It's surprising. (You're surprised.)

    o It feels like this might be a waste of your time, and so it frustrates you.

    o It almost feels like someone is out to get you, because every time you come in, there are these new surprises.

2. **Continue the paragraph.** The best reflections do not parrot back what the offender has said. They either paraphrase what has been said or guess what would come next if the offender continued to talk. In this way, good reflections give momentum to a conversation.

    o . . . and that makes you angry.

    o It feels pretty overwhelming when you think about how you're going to get the money to pay all these fees.

    o It feels to you like there are no good options here.

The following dialogues give several examples of response strategies that incorporate different types of reflections. In the first example, the offender minimizes the issue of his drinking and does not seem motivated to change:

> **Offender:** I don't know why this is such a big deal for everyone else. All my friends drink like I do.
>
> **Agent 1:** It doesn't seem like that big a deal, when what you see is people basically drinking like you do. *[Repeat—allows the offender to hear what he has said; rolls with resistance.]*
>
> **Agent 2:** Others have some concerns, but it hasn't been an issue for you. *[Rephrase—allows the offender to hear what he has said; rolls with resistance.]*

In the next example, the offender expresses frustration with the lack of success in his job search:

> **Offender:** Everyone should just relax. I'm doing the best I can with trying to find a job.
>
> **Agent:** It makes you angry because it feels like others aren't recognizing all the efforts you've made. *[Emotive—allows the offender to hear what he has said; rolls with resistance.]*

In this example, the offender expresses skepticism about his job search:

> **Offender:** I guess it would probably help me get a job, but . . .
>
> **Agent:** Part of you knows that finding a job would really help you out here, but at the same time, it's hard to think about how you're going to get the kind of job you want. *[Double-sided—points out mixed feelings or a contradiction in what the offender has said.]*

In a final example, the offender discusses drinking at family get-togethers:

> **Offender:** You don't know my family. It's basically impossible not to drink when we get together.
>
> **Agent:** It would be difficult to be around your family and not drink. It might even mean planning ahead to see how you might be able to manage that situation. *[Agreement with a twist—calls attention to one aspect of what the offender has said, and makes it more likely that the offender will continue to talk about that element.]*

Reflections help agents avoid two common problems. First, when there is a disagreement, the agent can be tempted to debate the issue with the offender. This persuasion strategy can create a situation where the agent gives the arguments for change, while the offender gives the arguments against change. Each leaves the interaction more convinced that he or she is right. The offender becomes convinced that change is unnecessary, and the agent becomes convinced that the offender is dragging his feet. To avoid these pitfalls, agents use reflections in two ways. The first is to roll with resistant comments instead of arguing with the offender. The second is to keep offenders talking in a particular direction to raise interest in change. The rest of this chapter talks about the first use; chapter 5 talks more about the second use.

Offenders may have conflicting feelings surrounding their behavior. An offender may recognize the negative effects of drug use on his family but, at the same time, enjoy getting high. It should not come as a surprise that an offender may feel two ways about supervision or may even be openly hostile to the idea of change. Allowing the offender to be resistant may require considerable patience on the part of the agent. Resistance is not necessarily a sign that things are going badly. Instead of confronting resistance, a more effective response is usually to reflect what the offender is saying and redirect the conversation with an open-ended question or a statement emphasizing personal responsibility.

**Offender:** It's impossible to find a good job. Nobody wants to hire a guy with a record.

**Agent 1:** There are lots of jobs out there, even for people on supervision. In fact, most offenders are able to find jobs. *[Confrontational—less effective.]*

**Agent 2:** It can be much more difficult for someone on supervision to find a job, sure. How do you think you might go about that? *[Reflective—more effective.]*

**Offender:** This is bullshit. Nobody told me I'd have to take those stupid classes. I got screwed by my lawyer.

**Agent 1:** You're the one on supervision! These classes are designed to help you with your anger—especially the kind of anger I'm seeing now. *[Confrontational—less effective.]*

**Agent 2:** You weren't expecting that you would have to attend these classes, and at this point it seems like a real waste of time. So maybe we can leave that for later. Here are the other things we've got to talk about . . . . Which one would you like to talk about? *[Reflective—more effective.]*

Reflections are also a good response when the agent does not know what to say. The agent is unlikely to do harm, and often can do much good, by reflecting what the offender is saying. The following dialogues present two examples of an agent restating what the offender has said and using reflections to avoid arguments over the offender's resistance to supervision conditions. In each case, the agent puts the burden for meeting those conditions back on the offender by giving him options and emphasizing his personal responsibility. In the first dialogue, the offender is surprised to learn that his supervision involves a significant amount of community service:

**Offender:** Community service? My lawyer didn't tell me I'd have to do that.

**Agent:** It's a bit of a surprise. *[Reflection—restatement.]*

**O:** Yeah, I don't think I should have to do that.

**A:** I understand that it's a surprise to you. We could certainly leave that for now, and talk about it at another meeting, and that would give you time to talk to your lawyer if you like. Would that be OK? *[Reflection—restatement; redirects conversation and gives option.]*

In the next dialogue, the offender resists making a change in his marijuana use. The agent avoids an argument by restating what the offender has said and emphasizing personal responsibility.

**Offender:** This whole thing is stupid. Sure, I smoke a little weed, but you're treating me like I'm some sort of addict or something.

**Agent:** It seems to you people might be blowing this out of proportion. *[Reflection—restatement.]*

**O:** Yeah, pot's not even a drug. It's all natural, it's an herb, so how can it be dangerous?

**A:** . . . and it doesn't seem to you like it's causing many problems. *[Reflection—continues the thought.]*

**O:** Yeah, everybody I know smokes. I'll be clean while I'm on supervision, but as soon as my 12 months is over, I'm going right back to smoking. They can't tell me what to do once I finish.

**A:** Well, of course, you have to decide what is right for you. I certainly can't tell you what to do after your supervision ends, but I do appreciate your willingness to stay clean while you're on supervision, even though it doesn't seem to you that it's a problem. *[Reflection—emphasizes personal responsibility.]*

**O:** Yeah, that's right. The judge is the one with the problem.

The agent does not allow the offender's irritating comments to put the agent on the defensive. The offender is already well aware of the court's/board's position, so the agent emphasizes the offender's personal responsibility given the conditions of supervision. At this moment, the offender may agree to complete a drug assessment, while still not admitting that he has a problem. Motivating the offender to complete this assessment may be a perfectly reasonable goal in a brief space of time, but at this point, a quick attitude shift is unlikely. The offender may need time to think about it.

Exhibit 4–2 presents examples of offenders' resistant comments and a few possible reflections for each. In each case, the reflections "roll with resistance" by restating the content or emotion of the comment. Reflections in these instances let the offender know that the agent has been listening. They allow the offender to save face and ultimately decrease the probability that he will continue to make similar statements.

In some instances, an agent may feel the need to confront an offender on some statement. However, the risk in using this harder approach is that it can increase resistance and close the door to more productive future conversations. Confrontational styles rarely engage people in thinking about behavior change. When offenders resist, it is usually better to back off, reflect, or try a different approach.

Although there is no hard and fast rule on what to reflect, the general principle is this: Reflect ambivalence in early interactions and emphasize change talk in later interactions. Similarly, reflect ambivalence early in an interview and emphasize change talk as the interview progresses. When in doubt, reflect what the offender is saying. (An exercise in rolling with resistance is provided at the end of this chapter.)

**Exhibit 4–2. Rolling With Resistance**

| Offender | Agent |
| --- | --- |
| This whole thing is about money! All you guys want is my money. | ■ It seems like maybe we care more about the money than we do your success on supervision. *[Restates offender's statement.]*<br><br>■ The whole money thing seems pretty overwhelming. *[Reflects emotion.]* |
| You've probably never even used drugs. How old are you anyway? I want a new officer. | ■ You feel like maybe I can't understand where you're coming from. *[Reflects emotion.]*<br><br>■ We can certainly look into that if that continues to be important to you. We definitely don't want to put up any barriers to successfully completing supervision. *[Gives option.]* |
| I wouldn't even have to do this community service if I had a different lawyer. | ■ It seems to you that things would have been different if you had had a different lawyer. *[Restates offender's statement.]*<br><br>■ Given that it is a condition of your probation, what do you what to do about that? *[Emphasizes personal responsibility.]* |

## Summarize What Has Been Said

A summary is a special form of reflection. Summaries remind the offender about major discussion points, the plan of action, and the offender's own reasons for taking action. Summaries are useful in two ways. If the offender slows or stops talking, summaries can act as a bridge to help him continue. Summaries may also help remind the offender what he has said or point out a connection between his statements.

In addition, summaries may allow for direction or commentary by the agent to emphasize elements or themes in what the offender has said. Summaries are also appropriate as transitions between major sections of an interview and at the end of an interview.

For instance, the following summaries make the transition between talking about payment of fees and the results of a recent urinalysis:

> **Agent:** Okay, it sounds like that will work for you. You said that you would be able to work an extra couple of hours a week, and your mom said she would be willing to set the money aside so you can get caught up on fees. I'd be glad to speak with her about that. That sounds like a good plan, and I really think it will help you out. One other thing we need to cover is the issue of the last UA. The lab results show that it came up diluted. This means that . . . .

> **Agent:** So at this point, it sounds like there's nothing we need to solve. The UA did come up dilute, but you're not reporting any use. This is the first time it's appeared this way, and I guess it's something to watch. We will definitely have to revisit this if it occurs again in the future. Since we haven't talked about this in a while, I wonder if it would be okay to spend a couple minutes talking about your past drug use, and maybe some of your reasons for wanting to stay clean now. Would that be okay?

Summaries often include such basic elements as:

- The specific problems or behaviors that were discussed.
- The offender's most important reasons for wanting to take action.
- What the plan of action will look like, including measures of success in completing the action and incentives or sanctions for completing or not completing the action.
- The date and time of the next contact.

Summaries may also help agents formulate their chronological records. A good summary shares many elements with a good chronological account. Both summarize what was said, include the offender's thoughts about motivation, and conclude with a plan of action. The following example summarizes and closes an early meeting focused on completing conditions related to anger management:

41

**Agent:** OK, so it looks like we're about out of time. We've been covering some of the conditions of your supervision. You thought that the fees would not be a problem, and we've agreed on a fee schedule. You thought it would just be easier to get the drug assessment out of the way, but at this point, you have some real mixed feelings about completing the batterer intervention class. You're aware that it's one of your conditions, but it's kind of costly, will take several weeks, and seems like it might be a waste of your time. That's certainly understandable, since it's a supervision order. We can revisit that next session if you want to take some time to think about it, and we can also talk about your community service options. I know this is a lot to cover in 20 minutes, but it I do appreciate your willingness to work with me. Is there anything else I need to know?

The next example summarizes a meeting focused on job placement:

**Agent:** We've talked about a couple of things today. One is catching up on your community service hours, and you thought that the parks and recreation option would work for you. Because they give double hours for weekend work, it's a way for you to get caught up quickly. As far as the employment situation, we talked about some of your other options. You thought that you would be able to put in five applications in the next 2 weeks, we talked about some options, and you have the verification forms for those. I don't want to be on your case about this—you have enough people lecturing you—except to remind you that you're approaching the end of your 90 days. If we can't verify employment, we move to weekly reporting, so that will mean that instead of reporting every month, you would report in every week. So where does this leave you?

How agents talk makes a difference in the way offenders react to the conditions of their supervision. The OARS techniques discussed above—open-ended questions, affirmations, reflections, and summaries—help gather information and set the stage for change. Although this chapter emphasizes these four techniques, the style of the interaction determines whether the techniques will work. In particular, the principles emphasized in earlier chapters—expressing empathy, rolling with resistance, developing discrepancy, and supporting self-efficacy—set the stage for a more productive interaction. Lists of questions and statements that may help in initiating and maintaining a motivational style are provided at the end of this chapter.

## An Example: Good Things and Not-So-Good Things

One way to broach the subject of change is to ask an offender about the benefits and drawbacks of a behavior. The two questions can be asked of almost anyone, no matter what his or her interest in change. They are also useful when an agent does not know what to say to an offender who has taken a very strong stance against change.

- What are some of the good things about . . . ?
- What are some of the not-so-good things about . . . ?

In this example, the questions focus on drinking:

**Agent:** In your experience, what have been some of the good things about drinking?

**Offender:** I don't know, I just like it. I guess it helps me to get along with people.

**A:** You enjoy the social part. What else do you like about it?

**O:** I guess I can forget about all the bad stuff in my life. It's like I can relax and just enjoy life.

**A:** So, for dealing with problems. Let me write that down. What else?

**O:** When my wife says something that pisses me off, and the kids are screaming, it just helps to calm me.

**A:** It's a way to deal with angry feelings. Okay. So if those are some of the good things, how about the other side. What have been some of the not-so-good things about drinking?

**O:** Well, it sucks to have a DWI [driving while intoxicated] on your record.

**A:** The DWI is definitely an example of one of the not-so-good things. What else?

First, the agent begins with an open-ended question (usually asking about the good things first) and immediately follows with a reflection. The agent continues to ask open-ended questions (e.g., "What else?") until the offender has listed several items. Most offenders can list several items on both sides, so the agent does not stop after the first or second item. Second, the agent does not shy away from asking about the good things about drinking. This agent is comfortable with the fact that drinking, like all problem behaviors, has some positive aspects. The agent is not condoning illegal or unhealthy behavior, but rather trying to understand the dilemma from the offender's perspective. The offender remains ambivalent about drinking, seeing both pros and cons, even though not drinking may be a condition of his supervision. Similarly, a sex offender may have mixed feelings about registering as a sex offender, even though it is a condition of his supervision. Third, the agent avoids labeling the behavior or using this exercise as a way to bully the offender into change. The questions invite the offender to talk on both sides of the issue; the offender gives both sides of the argument. The list resulting from this exchange might look something like this:

# CHAPTER 4

| Good Things About Drinking | Not-So-Good Things About Drinking |
|---|---|
| ■ Get along with friends. | ■ Legal trouble from DWI. |
| ■ Get away from problems. | ■ Trouble in marriage, wife nags me. |
| ■ Helps to deal with anger. | ■ Bad memories persist, increase. |
| | ■ Health, danger. |
| | ■ Possibility of another DWI. |
| | ■ Hangovers, blackouts. |
| | ■ Trouble at work. |
| | ■ Financial cost. |
| | ■ Bad role model for sons. |

The questions can also focus on the pros and cons of change itself. For instance, an agent might ask:

- What would be some of the benefits of quitting drug use?
- How about some of the drawbacks about quitting drug use? What would you have to give up?

Discussing the benefits and drawbacks of change gives the offender an opportunity to think about both sides of an issue. Many offenders remain stuck in destructive behavioral patterns simply because they have never taken the time to weigh the pros and cons of their behavior. At the same time, the agent gains information with which to tailor future conversations. The benefits of change tell the agent why the offender might want to make a change, and the drawbacks tell the agent the things the offender might have to give up or find substitutes for if he did decide to change. For instance, in the example given above, the offender recognizes that quitting drinking would save him from future legal difficulties, but at the same time, he wonders how he would deal with his anger or with whom he would spend time if he did not drink.

Although this exercise is designed to prepare the offender to begin thinking about change, the agent may immediately follow up on such a conversation in one of several ways. For instance, if the list of not-so-good things is longer than the list of good things, the agent might point this out and ask the offender what he makes of this discrepancy or what the next step is:

- It's interesting that your not-so-good thing list is longer than the good thing list. What do you make of that?
- What's the next step here?

Another followup technique is to ask about change hypothetically (see also chapter 5). If the offender chose not to drink, how might he still get some of the perceived benefits of drinking?

**Agent:** So, in thinking about the anger, if you decided not to drink, how else could you deal with these feelings of anger that keep coming up? What would that look like?

For an offender who has not yet decided to take action, this kind of question allows him to think about change without having to agree that he needs or wants to change. It is a safe but still productive question. Both of these followup techniques provide a bridge for connecting these questions to a discussion centered on changing a target behavior. A conversation about the good and not-so-good things might focus on the following:

- Continued drug or alcohol use.
- Obtaining GED or stable employment.
- Obtaining counseling for a chaotic family relationship.
- Continuing to associate with drug-using peers.
- Participating in a treatment group.
- Completing a drug or alcohol evaluation (whether or not the offender feels that drugs or alcohol are a problem).
- Attending anger management classes (whether or not the offender sees anger as a problem).
- Successfully completing supervision.

Focusing questions on future behavior sidesteps the issue of innocence or guilt, which can be particularly useful when an offender denies the offending behavior (see chapter 6). For instance, if an offender denies recent drug use, he may still be willing to discuss the pros and cons of drug use when he was using. Similarly, if a sex offender denies committing the offense, talking about the pros and cons of admitting to the offense or participating in treatment may still be productive. In both of these instances, talking about the pros and cons of a behavior given the conditions of supervision creates an alternative to debating innocence or guilt.

CHAPTER 4

## KEY POINTS

- Open-ended questions are better for increasing motivation—especially internal motivation—to change.

- Positive statements build rapport, provide feedback, and make positive behaviors more likely. Agents should use as many affirmations as possible and affirm any behavior that they want to see again.

- Reflections may repeat or rephrase what an offender has said, summarize an emotion, or point out mixed feelings. Reflections can also be used to respond when an agent does not know what to say.

- When reflecting, state only the most important elements of what the person has said.

- When offenders are resistant, it is usually better to back off, reflect, or try a different approach.

- How the agent talks with offenders makes a difference in the way they react to the agent and to the conditions of their supervision. Confrontational statements that defend the court's/board's position are unlikely to persuade the offender.

- An MI-inclined agent understands that all problem behaviors have some positive aspects and allows the offender to talk about both sides of the issue.

## Exercise: Rolling With Resistance

All of the following are things a client might say. Think of two things you might say in response if you want to roll with the resistance.

You might try—

- Simple reflection (restating content in similar words).
- Paraphrased reflection (restating content in other words or inferring meaning).
- Emotive reflection (stating the emotion).
- Double-sided reflection (highlighting mixed feelings).
- Asking a hypothetical question (If you wanted to, how…?).

1. I'm not the one with the problem. If I drink, it's because my wife is always nagging me.

2. You'd drink, too, if you had a family like mine.

3. I know you're sitting there thinking that I'm an addict, but it's not like that. I just like getting high sometimes.

4. My wife is always exaggerating! I never hurt anybody when I was drinking!

5. The job isn't my problem. What I want to talk about is my son—now he's the one with the problem!

## Useful Questions for Motivational Interviews

What concerns do you (does your wife, girlfriend, etc.) have?

How has . . . caused trouble for you?

What are some good things about . . . ? What are some not-so-good things about . . . ?

How would things be better for you if you made that change?

What thoughts have you had about change?

What do you think will happen if you don't . . . ?

If there were no more drugs or alcohol in the world, what do you think would replace how drugs make you feel?

If you look forward to, say, a year from now, how would you want your life to be different?

How do you want things to end up when you're done with probation? Where do you want to be?

How would that pay off for you, if you went ahead and made this change?

In what situations is it hardest for you to stay sober?

There are a few things that might work for you (provide a short list). Which of these would you like to try?

Here are some things that we need to talk about (provide a short list). Which of these would you like to talk about first?

On a scale of 1 to 10, how important is it for you to change your . . . ?

On a scale of 1 to 10, how confident are you that you could change if you wanted to?

If you wanted to change, how would you go about it?

Who would (or will) help you to . . . ?

What worked for you in the past?

What would you like to work on first?

When would be a good time to start?

How could (or will) you do that?

How can you make that happen?

What can I do to help you succeed at . . . ?

What else?

## Useful Statements for Motivational Interviews

Thanks for coming in on time.

It feels to you that people might be blowing this out of proportion.

You don't feel like I can understand where you're coming from.

At this point, it doesn't seem that big a deal to you.

Drinking has some positive aspects for you.

It's frustrating. (You're frustrated with having to be here.)

It's difficult. (I know this must be difficult for you.)

It's hard for you. (It might be hard for you.)

I can see why you might think that.

So the thing that most concerns you is . . . .

You want to do the right thing.

That's a good idea.

I think you could do it if you really wanted to.

I think that will work for you.

Thanks for talking with me.

I appreciate your honesty.

Restatement of anything that indicates concerns about present behavior or interest in change.

# CHAPTER 5

# Building Motivation for Change

Whereas the last chapter focused on listening skills, this chapter talks about ways to tip the motivational balance toward change. The chapter begins by presenting strategies for guiding a conversation to focus on behavior change. It then suggests ways to encourage positive talk and engage the offender in thinking about change. Finally, the chapter suggests ways to help connect talk to action.

## Pick a Focus

Conversations about change are most effective when they address one or two areas at a time. Thus, it is important for the agent to decide which behaviors deserve consideration at this moment and which can be left for later. Agents must weigh issues based on their importance to the court/board as well as to the offender.

Early on, assessment results or a case plan may suggest areas of focus. For instance, a risk/needs assessment helps determine the kinds of services provided to an offender, including monitoring, placement, and specific areas of change. The following example illustrates focusing the discussion of the results of the risk/needs assessment:

> **Agent:** What we have here are the results from one of your assessments. It shows different areas that might make it easier or harder for you to successfully complete supervision. Some areas you don't have any control over. For instance, we can't change the fact that you've been convicted before or that you've had a previous probation revoked. On the other hand, some things you do have control over. Three areas that we'll be revisiting are your living situation, your marital relationship, and your circle of friends. All three of these seem to have gotten you in trouble in the past, or at least made it difficult for you to keep out of trouble. I wonder if you could tell me a little about each of these areas. For instance, I'm interested to know how your circle of friends might have caused trouble for you in the past.

Chapter 7 talks more about ways to integrate assessment and case planning into subsequent interactions. Later on, supervision progress or continued problem may determine areas of focus. In this example, the agent transitions from asking questions to talking about a substance abuse evaluation:

**Agent:** OK, I think I have what I need for my case notes. Thanks for answering those questions. There's a couple of things I'd like to talk about today. One of your conditions requires that you complete a substance abuse evaluation in the first 90 days, and I'm concerned that you have about a month left to get that done to avoid a sanction. Would it be OK if we talked about that for a minute? Tell me this, on a scale of 1 to 10, how important is it for you to make this happen in the next week or so? *[See "question on a scale" technique later in this chapter.]*

Another way to focus is to ask the offender to set the agenda. Supervising agents cannot always negotiate "if" a person will comply with the terms of his supervision, but they can usually negotiate "how" and "why" the person will comply. In transitioning from asking questions to talking about a substance abuse evaluation, giving the offender a choice in what to talk about can be a good strategy for encouraging him to become more involved in his own plan of action:

**Agent:** We've been working on a couple of things. One is your community service, and the second is completing this anger management class. We also need to make sure you are staying current with your fees, which will probably mean talking about how the job search is going. Which of those would you like to talk about?

## Look For and Emphasize Things That Motivate

Legal sanctions may motivate some people, but in general, the power of external punishment as a motivator is overestimated. The most powerful motivators are intrinsic: family, children, friends, keeping a job, gaining the respect of others, or feeling a measure of control over life. For most people, change is an inside job.

## Ask Questions That Raise Interest

Chapter 4 talked about using open-ended questions to encourage an offender to think and talk about change. The following questions, based on the DARN–C (desire, ability, reasons, needs, commitment) model discussed in chapter 3, address the offender's reasons for change:

- **Drawbacks of current behavior:**
    o What concerns do you have about your drug use?
    o What concerns does your wife have about your drug use?
    o What has your drug use cost you?

- **Benefits of change:**
    - If you went ahead and took care of that class, how would that make things better for you?
    - You talk a lot about your family. How would finding a job benefit your family?
    - How would that make things better for your kids?

- **Desire to change:**
    - How badly do you want that?
    - How does that make you feel?
    - How would that make you feel different?

- **Ability to change:**
    - How would you do that if you wanted to?
    - What would that take?
    - If you did decide to change, what makes you think you could do it?

- **Specific commitments the offender will make to change:**
    - How are you going to do that?
    - What will that look like?
    - How are you going to make sure that happens?

Because questions partially determine the offender's responses, the agent asks questions that try to elicit increased motivation and commitment to change. When talking about matters of fact, this might be considered leading, but when talking about motivation, the agent can assume that every offender has some mixed feelings regarding the desired behavior changes. The outcome is not fixed, so the agent provides every opportunity for the offender to talk and think about positive behavior change.

In guiding a conversation toward change, it is usually better to start by exploring the offender's mixed feelings. Later, it is usually better to follow up on elements that express desire to change, ability to change, or reasons for change. Once an offender has decided to take action, it can be appropriate to ask questions about commitment to change.

### Follow Up on Productive Talk

A second way to keep the conversation focused on change is to emphasize productive offender statements, ignoring less productive statements unless there is a good reason to address them. Consider the following statement from a domestic violence offender:

**Offender:** Sure, counseling would probably help us a lot. But there's no way my wife would go for it. And anyway, we can't afford it.

In this statement, the offender is saying at least three things: first, counseling might help improve their relationship; second, his wife is reluctant to participate; and third, it might be too expensive. What the officer says next determines which of these three elements the offender talks about. Of the three, the first is probably the most likely to be productive. Following up on either of the other two elements, which are negative, encourages the person to talk about barriers to change and probably will not make change more likely.

At least two options for following up on the first element are available. One option is to begin raising the offender's interest or readiness to engage in treatment; another is to talk about planning independent of desire. For instance, a question or reflection might highlight the person's desire to obtain help:

- It sounds like there are some barriers there, but it also sounds like part of you thinks that counseling would really help.
- In what ways do you think it would help?
- What problems would that solve?

Another type of question might ask about why or how he might obtain help:

**Agent:** Let's say for a moment your wife was on board. How would you go about getting some help here? What would work for you?

Here is an example of an offender who expresses a desire for change but comes up with excuses for not changing his behavior:

**Offender:** I want to stay clean and sober, but I can't get a job because of this court thing and so I have to live with my brother who drinks all the time.

The temptation for the agent is to answer the part that is most irritating—the suggestion that the court has ruined the probationer's job prospects and placed him at risk for relapse. However, the most productive element for increasing the probationer's interest in change is his stated desire to remain clean and sober. The agent might respond with a reflection or question that focuses on this element:

- You do want to stay clean and sober.
- How are you going to manage that?
- You really do want to do the right thing here. But given that you've been placed in a difficult position, how are you going to make sure you stay clean?

The following two dialogues present examples of how an agent can use questions and statements to draw out more productive elements in talking with offenders who are in different stages of motivation to change. In both dialogues, the agent uses reflections and questions to shift the conversation toward change. In the first dialogue, the offender minimizes the issue of his drug use and shows little motivation to change.

> **Offender:** Sure, I smoke pot every once in a while. Everyone else is all concerned, but I don't think it's that big a deal. I mean, don't a lot of people smoke?
>
> **Agent:** So, some other people are concerned, but it doesn't seem like a big issue to you. You think that maybe they're blowing the whole thing out of proportion. *[Reflection—simple restatement of concerns.]*
>
> **O:** Yeah, I'm old enough to make my own decisions. It's not like I'm stealing or anything to buy drugs.
>
> **A:** So, who is concerned about the use? *[Open question—asks about others' concerns.]*
>
> **O:** My mom for one. But it's no big deal. She doesn't know what's going on with me anyway. And she smokes too. She's such a hypocrite.
>
> **A:** What do you think she's afraid of? *[Open question—asks for elaboration on concerns.]*

In the second dialogue, the offender has relapsed into drug use but demonstrates some interest in changing his behavior.

> **Offender:** I don't know what happened. It's just like the last time. Things are going well, and then I'm using again.
>
> **Agent:** It's almost like it sneaks up on you when you least expect it. We talked about how much you wanted to remain clean, because you recognize the negative effect on your kids. You see it. *[Reflection—restates drawbacks of use, desire to remain abstinent.]*
>
> **O:** Yeah, they see it too. It's never long before I'm using in front of them, and that's not right.
>
> **A:** You want to do right by your kids. You don't want them to have that same environment which has caused you all this trouble. *[Reflection—restates reasons for abstinence.]*
>
> **O:** There's got to be something better than this. Maybe some more of those classes or something.
>
> **A:** Maybe getting some formal treatment would help. *[Reflection—restates desire to change, adds treatment element.]*

CHAPTER 5

### Use Forward-Focused Questions

When talking about action, it can be more efficient to concentrate on forward-focused questions. Forward-focused questions ask what the offender could do or will do or what things will work for him. This is in contrast to backward-focused questions that ask about why the offender can't, won't, or didn't do something. The following example presents contrasting responses to backward- and forward-focused questions in following up with a domestic violence offender who must attend a drug and alcohol assessment, even though the incident did not involve alcohol.

> **Offender:** Alcohol assessment? I don't even drink! I don't have time to do that.

> **Agent 1:** Why can't you do that? *[Backward-focused question.]*
>
> **Agent 2:** How could you do that? *[Forward-focused question.]*

> **O:** I wasn't even drinking when it happened. Plus, it's just going to create more trouble if my wife thinks I have a drinking problem.
>
> **O:** Well, I guess I could go this weekend when I'm off work, but I still think the thing is a waste of time.

The first agent's question sets up the offender to give a list of barriers; the second agent's question encourages the offender to think of solutions. The second agent's question also sidesteps a debate about whether the offender has a "problem" with alcohol. This offender may agree to complete the assessment even though he still does not admit he has an alcohol problem. Motivating the offender toward this action may be a reasonable goal, given a brief space of time. Exhibit 5–1 presents a series of backward-focused questions transformed into forward-focused questions.

**Exhibit 5–1.** Transforming Backward-Focused to Forward-Focused Questions

| Avoid Backward-Focused Questions | Try Forward-Focused Questions |
| --- | --- |
| I thought we agreed that you would get information on that AA group. What was the problem? | AA will probably be an important part of successfully completing supervision, so I'm wondering how we can make sure that will happen this week. |
| You're late with that receipt for your payment. Why didn't you bring that in? | You're late with a receipt for your payment, and I'm wondering if there's something that we can problem-solve here. How can we make sure that you get it to me this week? |
| Why couldn't you get a copy of that job application? | How can we make sure that I can get a copy of that application by the time we meet next week? |

Although identifying obstacles is an important aspect of planning, the downside is that this tack tends to draw out excuses. This approach also increases the interaction time because the agent must revisit the issue of how the offender can or will accomplish the task. Problem solving also assumes a motivated subject; given a short amount of time, it is usually better to put the effort into building motivation and to leave the primary responsibility for problem solving with the offender.

## Ask Scaled (Rather Than Yes/No) Questions

One way to structure a brief discussion about change is to ask scaled questions about different aspects of motivation—being "ready, willing, and able" (Rollnick 1998). The following questions show how these aspects relate back to specific DARN–C elements:

- **Desire (will) to change.**
  On a scale of 1 to 10, how important is it for you to make a change in . . . ?

- **Ability (confidence) to change.**
  On a scale of 1 to 10, how confident are you that you could make a change in . . . ?

- **Readiness (specific commitment) to change.**
  On a scale of 1 to 10, how ready are you to make a change in . . . ?

There are two advantages to asking questions in this way. First, a scaled question captures ambivalence better than a yes/no question. A person who says, "I don't need to do anything about that" might give a two or three in response to a scaled question. Second, a scaled response is more useful for initiating a conversation about change; it assumes at least a minimal willingness to change, whereas a "yes/no" question may appear to close off the possibility of change entirely (see exhibit 5–2). To aid in case planning, use the separate importance and confidence rulers shown in exhibit 5–3 to talk about readiness to complete different mandated conditions.

**Exhibit 5–2.** Transforming Yes/No Questions to Scaled Questions

| Avoid Yes/No (Closed) Questions | Try Scaled (Open-Ended) Questions |
|---|---|
| If you want to keep custody of your kids, you need to find a job. Isn't that what you want? | On a scale of 1 to 10, how important is it to keep custody of your kids? Why is that? |
| Do you want to complete supervision? | On a scale of 1 to 10, how important is it to you to complete supervision? Why is that? Why not a lower number? |
| Don't you want to do something about your drug use? Can't you see what it's doing to your family? | On a scale of 1 to 10, how ready are you to do something about the drug use? Why is that? Why not a lower number? |

**Exhibit 5–3. Importance and Confidence Rulers**

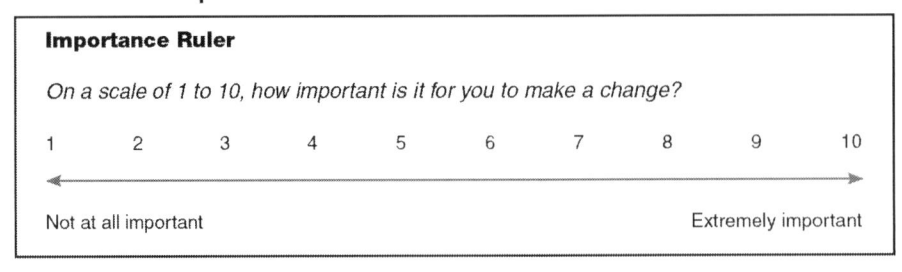

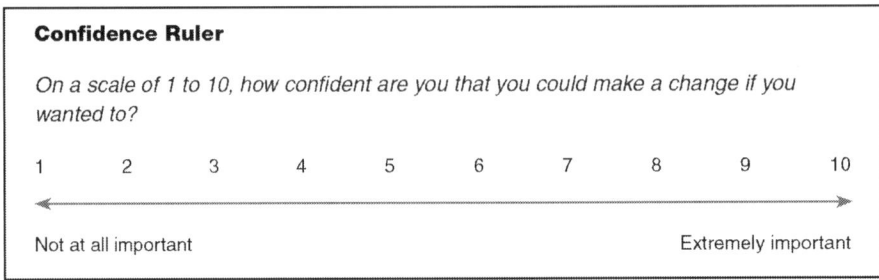

**Importance Ruler**

*On a scale of 1 to 10, how important is it for you to make a change?*

1   2   3   4   5   6   7   8   9   10

⟵—————————————————————————⟶

Not at all important                          Extremely important

**Confidence Ruler**

*On a scale of 1 to 10, how confident are you that you could make a change if you wanted to?*

1   2   3   4   5   6   7   8   9   10

⟵—————————————————————————⟶

Not at all important                          Extremely important

Beyond the assessment question, some subtlety in followup questions can be helpful. If the goal is to raise interest or confidence, concentrate followup questions in a certain direction (e.g., "Why not a lower number?"). This encourages the offender to elaborate on why change is important and why he is confident that he can do it. Followup questions also provide a springboard for talking about a plan of action. If it is important to the offender, what is he willing to do to make it happen?

The steps in using importance and confidence questions look like this:

**Importance questions:**

- **Ask how important it is to make a change in an area.**
  On a scale from 1 to 10, how important is it for you to make a change in your . . . ?

- **Reflect the response.**
  It's pretty important (somewhat important) for you . . . .

- **Ask for elaboration.**
  Why is that? What things make it important?

- **Ask why not a lower number.**
  Why did you pick a five and not a one?

- **Ask for elaboration.**
  Tell me more about that. What else? . . . What else?

# BUILDING MOTIVATION FOR CHANGE

**Confidence questions:**

- **Ask how confident the offender is in his ability to change.**
  On a scale from 1 to 10, how confident are you that you could make a change if you wanted to?

- **Reflect the response.**
  You're pretty confident (somewhat confident, not very confident) that you could . . . .

- **Ask for elaboration.**
  Why is that? What things make you confident?

- **Ask why not a lower number.**
  Why did you pick a five and not a one?

- **Ask for elaboration.**
  Tell me more about that. What else? . . . What else?

The next dialogues present examples of followup questions to three different offender responses to scaled importance and confidence questions directed to building motivation to avoid drug use. The first dialogue presents responses to a scaled importance question:

**Agent:** On a scale of 1 to 10, how important is it for you to stay clean?

**Offender 1:** A one.

**A:** OK, so it's not that important to you at this time. Let me remind you though, that it is one of your conditions of supervision. Maybe we can visit that later.

**Offender 2:** About a four.

**A:** So, about in the middle. But I'm wondering, why did you say a four and not a one? So, one reason it's important is . . . . What else?

**Offender 3:** Maybe a nine.

**A:** So it's very important for you to avoid using drugs. Why is that? What else?

The second dialogue presents responses to a scaled confidence question:

**Agent:** Using the same scale, how confident are you that you could stay clean if you wanted to?

**Offender 1:** A one.

**A:** Hmmm . . . Pretty low. What would it take to raise that estimate a little bit? Tell me about a change you made in the past. How did you go about it? Who might help you to . . . ?

**Offender 2:** About a four.

**A:** So, about in the middle. But why a four and not a one? What else? What would it take to raise your confidence to, say, an eight? How would you go about it? How can I help you to make that happen?

**Offender 3:** A ten.

**A:** Very confident. How would you go about it? What would it look like? What else? How can I help you make that happen?

Scaled questions can be used to talk about any current behavior or area in need of change. For instance:

On a scale of 1 to 10, how important is it to—

- Complete community service hours?
- Get caught up on fees?
- Avoid contact with the victim?
- Complete a batterer intervention course?
- Complete a substance abuse evaluation?

Scaled questions can also be used to capture more general motivation to complete supervision successfully:

On a scale of 1 to 10, how important is it to complete all of your conditions of supervision successfully?

As with the other interviewing techniques presented in this guide, this technique is not meant to be used to bully offenders. (An agent was once heard to say to an offender, "On a scale of 1 to 10, would you rather spend 6 months in jail or 12 months?") These questions are designed to access internal motivation for change. In general, bullying offenders with external threats makes it less likely that they will take on new, more prosocial behaviors. An exercise in asking good questions and additional examples of good communication are provided at the end of this chapter.

## Strengthen Commitment To Change

The agent hopes that at some point, the balance of motivation will shift. He/she spends time exploring the offender's ambivalence and building motivation to help the offender decide what he would like to do about his situation. Exhibit 5–4 shows these two phases of motivation. Phase 1 corresponds to the early stages of change, when the agent works to elicit talk about desire, ability, reasons, and need for change. ("Why is change important?") Phase 2 occurs when the agent works to elicit specific commitments from an offender who is motivated to change. ("What do you want to do about it?")

A domestic violence offender might begin supervision not believing that his anger issues are important. In exploring the issue with his supervising agent, he may become more aware of the way his behavior affects himself or others. The agent looks for statements like the following from the offender to show that the balance is ready to shift from Phase 1 to Phase 2:

- The cops keep showing up, and it's embarrassing.
- Things have gotten really bad between us. I don't know what's going to happen.

**Exhibit 5–4.** Two Phases of Motivation

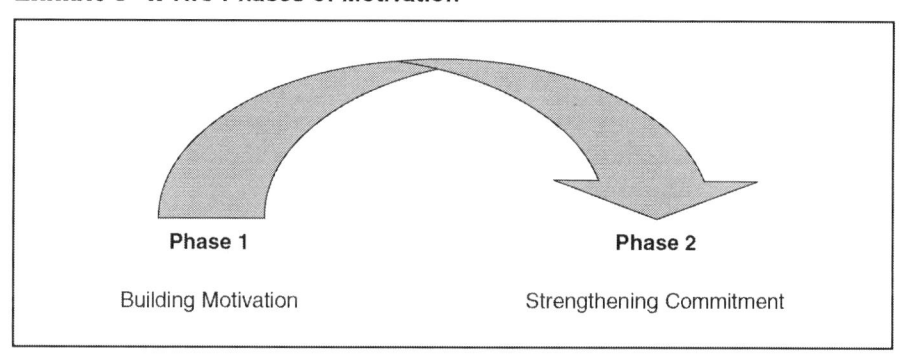

Phase 1 — Building Motivation
Phase 2 — Strengthening Commitment

- She really gets onto me about coming home late, and I guess I don't handle it that well.
- I guess I should just take that anger management class, even though I don't think I really need it.

In these statements, the offender is expressing desire, ability, reasons, or need to change (Phase 1). Given these signals, an agent can move the conversation toward commitment (Phase 2) by asking an action question, giving advice or information, or asking about change without obtaining a specific commitment.

## Ask an Action Question

One way to move the conversation toward commitment is to ask an action question:

- Where do we go from here?
- What's the next step?
- What do you want to do about that?
- What's one thing you would be willing to do this week to make that happen, or is this something you need more time to think about?

An action question not only moves the conversation toward change, but it also gauges the respondent's level of commitment. If the respondent answers with weak commitment language, the agent can either proceed with this weak commitment or continue to elicit change talk until the respondent is ready to make a stronger commitment.

## Give Advice Without Telling What To Do

Another way to move the interaction toward commitment is to provide information or advice without obtaining a specific commitment from the offender. Because most supervision interactions are relatively brief, many agents suggest how the offender might go about securing transportation, finding a job, or completing community service hours. However, a person is much more likely to act on a solution he comes up with himself. Suggestions are sometimes helpful in changing behavior, but the danger is that an offender may be less likely to consider them if he feels that he is being told what to do. Therefore, agents should be careful to avoid rushing to provide too many suggestions.

In the following interaction, the offender has not been able to complete his community service referral because of transportation difficulties. Each suggestion by the agent for resolving those difficulties meets with objections from the offender:

**Offender:** I'm trying to get there, but I don't have a car.

**Agent:** What about borrowing a car from your mother?

**O:** My mother doesn't even know I'm on supervision. There's no way I could ask her. She'd totally freak out!

**A:** How about the bus line?

**O:** Yeah, I thought about that, but there's no bus line near my house.

**A:** Well, how did you get here today?

**O:** My buddy dropped me off, but he doesn't live anywhere near the place you told me to go.

This agent has fallen into a classic trap. The agent gives a suggestion, and the offender tells why it will not work for him. The interaction frustrates both parties. The agent feels like the offender must be dragging his feet, and the offender feels like the agent does not understand his situation. Certainly, transportation is a real barrier for many people. And yet, most people seem to figure out how to accomplish things that are important to them. One simple tool is to ask the offender what ideas he has for accomplishing that task or what things have worked for him in the past.

Agents sometimes do decide to provide advice. In such instances, the following strategies will make it more likely that the person will seriously listen to and act on that advice:

- **Ask for permission before providing advice.**
  Would it be okay if I gave you some information about . . . ?

- **Preface advice with permission to disagree.**
  This may or may not work for you, but one thing you might think about is . . . .

- **Give more than one option.**
  There are a couple of things that might work for you here.

- **Emphasize personal responsibility.**
  Ultimately, you're the one who has to decide how this goes. You'll have to decide what's right for you—whether it's easier to make this happen, even though it's not convenient, or whether it's just easier to take the sanction.

The following example using these strategies demonstrates how the previous dialogue might have gone differently:

**Offender:** I'm trying to get there, but I don't have a car.

**Agent:** It sounds like it might be difficult for you.

**O:** Yeah, how am I supposed to get all the way over there without a car? I mean, are you going to come pick me up?

**A:** It sounds like it is something you want to do, but at the same time you're frustrated in thinking about how you're going to get there without a car. It does make things more difficult.

**O:** Yeah, I want to. I just don't know how.

**A:** I wonder if you would be interested in working together to come up with a solution. Is that something you would be interested in?

**O:** Yeah, I guess.

**A:** There are a couple of things that might work for you here . . . .

The second dialogue will take more time because the agent is listening to the offender and encouraging him to work out his own solution. Exhibit 5–5 illustrates the difference between less effective responses that dictate a solution and more effective responses that help an offender to come up with his own solution.

**Exhibit 5–5.** Responses That Facilitate Rather Than Dictate Solutions

| Dictating Solutions | Facilitating Solutions |
| --- | --- |
| Couldn't you borrow your mother's car? | So it's going to be very important for you to keep your meetings. How are you going to make that happen? |
| What about that job at McDonald's? | McDonald's might be one option, but I'm wondering what else you've thought of? |
| The next time you get angry, make sure you count to 10 before acting. | When you think about times when you've been able to manage your anger, what things have worked for you? |

A menu of options is another way to provide suggestions. If the agent provides several options instead of just one, it is more likely that the offender will find an option that works for him:

- What are your options here?
- You have a couple of options here . . . .
- I know transportation has been a problem for you, so here are a few things that might work. (Provides a short list.) Which would you like to check into?
- We have a few things we need to talk about: the job situation, taking care of the drug education class, and getting caught up on fees. Which would you like to talk about first?

The three previous sections have talked about ways to move the conversation from motivation (Phase 1) to commitment (Phase 2). However, it is important to recognize that individuals may go back and forth between the phases. They may express interest in change while talking about the barriers to change. Ambivalence is a normal part of the change process, even after someone has decided to act. The next set of dialogues illustrate some ways that an agent can respond to an offender who continues to have mixed feelings about change.

**Offender 1:** Yeah, I want to find a job, but who's going to take care of my kids while I'm working?

**Agent 1:** It might be hard for you. *[Reflects offender's ambivalence about change.]*

**Offender 2:** I'll go to the class, but I still think my wife's the one with the problem.

**Agent 2:** Ultimately, I guess you'll have to decide whether you're willing to take action here. *[Emphasizes personal responsibility.]*

**Offender 3:** I just don't know how I can afford to make the restitution payments.

**Agent 3:** I know it seems pretty overwhelming. I'm wondering whether it would be helpful to spend a minute looking over this finance worksheet. I'd be glad to talk with you to see if we can come up with a plan. *[Offers assistance.]*

### Help Connect Talk to Action

The final step is to talk about the specifics of the plan for changing the offender's behavior and meeting the supervision requirements. The more specifically an offender talks about this plan, the more likely he is to follow through with it. If an offender agrees to attend Alcoholics Anonymous, what kind of group will he attend? When is the meeting? With whom will he go? How will attendance be monitored? Because of time constraints, the tendency is to give the offender the plan. However, offender speech is a much better predictor of action than agent speech. For this reason, agents go out of their way to encourage an offender to develop and talk about his own plan, addressing the following issues:

- What specifically will the behavior look like?
- When will the behavior occur?

- Where will the behavior will occur?
- Why is the behavior personally important to the offender?
- How can the behavior be achieved? How can the agent verify action? How can the agent assist in carrying out the plan?

Using written or visual cues, such as handouts or worksheets, can be helpful. Some people work well with a simple plan of action. In the following example, the behavior is job seeking:

- **What?**
  Submit five job applications before next meeting.
- **When?**
  I can go any day, but Tuesday mornings after the drug class are best.
- **Where?**
  Mostly fast food applications, but I might also try supermarket checker positions.
- **Why?**
  I would have my own income, and maybe be able to move out on my own. I might be able to be dismissed from supervision early.
- **How?**
  My mom can take me to get the applications. I can bring the job applications and copy them at the department office. Officer can assist me by calling on Tuesday morning to remind me.

The better the foundation the agent has laid for change, the easier the solution will appear. In fact, some of the best interactions are those where an agent has spent a good deal of time helping the offender to explore why it is personally important to complete a condition. If the offender decides it is important, the agent can then ask for a commitment: "How are you going to make that happen?" It is amazing to see barriers disappear when an offender is well prepared for change.

## KEY POINTS

- Prioritize issues based on importance. Use assessment results or a case plan to guide the focus, or let the offender pick from a list.

- Threats of punishment rarely produce lasting behavior change. Raising internal motivation involves recognizing and encouraging the kind of talk that increases that motivation.

- Follow up on productive statements and ignore less productive statements.

- Ask scaled questions rather than yes/no questions.

- Spend time building motivation and then ask an action question about what the offender will do.

- A person is more likely to act on a solution he feels he came up with. Involve the offender in planning, use a menu of options, and give advice without bullying.

- The more specifically a person talks about the plan, the more likely he is to follow through with it.

## Exercise: Asking Good Questions

Not-so-good questions increase resistance and decrease the likelihood that the offender will talk about changes in his behavior. Many not-so-good questions are suggestions (or accusations) in disguise. For each of the not-so-good questions below, rephrase the question to reduce resistance and encourage talk about change.

| Not-So-Good Question | Better Question |
|---|---|
| You don't have a drinking problem, do you? | |
| What about the job training program. Could you do that? | |
| If you got a job, wouldn't that make things better at home? | |
| Aren't you worried about how your drug use affects your kids? | |
| Every time you see Larry, it seems like you get in trouble. What about driving home another way so that you can avoid running into him? | |
| Why can't you just get a ride to the AA meeting with your brother? | |
| You use again, you go to jail. Is that what you want? | |
| Is your wife concerned about you being on probation? | |

## Communication Examples

Some statements and questions are better than others because they increase the chance that the offender will talk more productively about change.

| Trap | What NOT To Say | What TO Say |
| --- | --- | --- |
| **Playing the Expert** | You don't have a job because you're not putting in enough applications. | What ideas do you have as to how you might get a job? |
| **Arguing the Positive Side** | You need to stop making excuses and find a job. | How would things be better for you if you found a job? |
| **Giving Unsolicited Advice** | You need to get up first thing in the morning, get a cup of coffee, and go in to fill out that application. | If you decided you wanted to put in a job application, how would you go about that? |
| **Premature Focus on Change** | We've been talking a lot about how important it is to get a job, and this week I'd like you to submit five job applications. | Ultimately you're the one who has to decide whether you want to put in the hard work to finding a job. What do you think is a reasonable number of applications to put in this week? |
| **Asking Backward-Focused Questions** | Why did you go to that party when you knew it was going to get you in trouble?<br><br>Why haven't you been able to get a job? | It sounds like that situation really got you in trouble.<br><br>What can you do this week to move this thing forward? |

# CHAPTER 6

# Navigating Tough Times: Working With Deception, Violations, and Sanctions

In dealing with offenders, probation and parole officers must play two conflicting roles—counselor and mentor to the offender and representative of the justice system who has the power to return the offender to confinement. Probation and parole officers help the offender plan to meet supervision conditions, but dispense sanctions if he fails; they ask the offender to be honest, but also report violations to a court or board (Trotter 1999). This chapter suggests ways to navigate this dual role—to address violations and supervise for compliance while maintaining a motivational style.

## Lying and Deception

Deception is commonplace in criminal justice, whether by deliberate lies, half-truths, or omission of information. In response to being charged with a violation or significant lack of progress, offenders sometimes lie ("I didn't do it!") or make excuses for their behavior ("I did it but it's not so bad"). The range of assertions seems endless: "Everybody does it" (consensus); "It's not that bad" (minimization); "I needed the money" (justification); "I didn't mean to" (intention). With the coercion inherent in corrections, it is reasonable for probation and parole officers to expect deception from a certain percentage of the offenders whom they supervise. At the same time, it is important to understand that most offenders bend the truth for pretty ordinary reasons. To some extent, lying and deception—hiding our inner selves or our outer behavior—are simply part of our social world. Lying is one more natural continuum of human behavior. It is not so much its presence or absence, but the degree of deception that becomes a problem.

## Why Do People Lie?

This chapter talks about two types of deception: Intentional, self-aware deception toward others and deception toward others that also involves some degree of self-deception.

# CHAPTER 6

People tend to make two assumptions about their own actions (Sigmon and Snyder 1993): "I'm a good person" and "I am in control most of the time." These assumptions protect and enhance mental health. These beliefs also mean that people may speak in a way that protects these assumptions. For instance:

- **A person will lie to save face.** To save face is to protect a positive self-image—"I am a good person" and "I am in control."

- **A person will lie to save face for someone he or she cares about.** Relationships are powerful motivators. This explains why abused children may lie to a protective services worker to protect their parent(s) and why one spouse cannot be compelled to testify against the other in a court of law. It creates a conflict to have to provide damaging information about someone with whom one has a close relationship.

- **A person will lie to prevent a perceived loss of freedom or resources.** There are penalties for admitting lawbreaking behavior, and an offender must weigh the immediate penalties resulting from telling the truth against the possibly worse, but less certain, penalties that might occur if he told a lie. In fact, a lie can be a good gamble if the immediate penalties are more certain and possibly just as bad.

Any or all of these influences might be present as an offender progresses through the system. Like all people, offenders have obligations—to personal pride, important relationships, or the threat of a loss of freedom—that they must weigh against what the system is asking of them.

There are also deceptive tendencies that operate partially outside the offender's awareness—ways that people bend information to make it more consistent with how they feel or what they believe (Saarni and Lewis, 1993):

- **A person will reinterpret information so that it fits with his basic assumptions about his goodness or competency.** Nowhere is this more evident than in making excuses. For instance, if I believe that I am generally competent, but I am not able to follow through with a referral, I tend to believe that circumstances must have made it too difficult. Taking full responsibility for poor outcomes can conflict with perceptions of oneself as good and in control.

- **A person will bend information in response to who is asking the question and how the question is phrased.** How an agent asks a question partially determines what answer the offender gives. In fact, some agents inadvertently encourage lies through their use of questions. In an attempt to trick an offender into admitting something, they will ask the offender to elaborate on an obviously concocted story. In listening to himself, the offender comes to defend, justify, or perhaps even believe elements of that story. It becomes more difficult for him to extricate himself once he has created details—new lies—to support his initial story. Other agents push offenders to justify past or present behavior by asking backwards-focused questions such as, "Why didn't you do that?" or "Why can't you do that?" In response to questions like these, the agent essentially gets what he or she has asked for—a list of excuses for why the offender was not able to complete some task, interpreted in a way that fits with the offender's basic beliefs about his own goodness and autonomy.

## What Can Be Done About It?

First, the adage "Don't take it personally" is appropriate here. Taking full responsibility for poor outcomes can conflict with a person's perceptions of himself or herself as good and in control. Many offenders deceive not so much to con the agent as to defend these assumptions within themselves—it may be a product of self-deception.

Fortunately, a positive relationship between the agent and the offender makes lies less likely. Some agents believe that a confrontational style sends the offender a message that the agent cannot be taken in, but research suggests it is more the opposite: a harsh, coercive style can prompt an offender to lie to save face and allows the offender to justify his lies to himself. Agents who have positive, collaborative relationships with offenders are less likely to be lied to. A mutual working style makes honesty more likely. A motivational approach handles deception, not by ignoring it or getting agitated by it, but rather by taking a step back from the debate.

## Addressing Violations and Sanctions

When faced with difficult situations, the temptation for the agent is to move to one side or the other—to become too harsh or too friendly—when a more middle-of-the-road approach is called for. Agents are like facilitators or consultants in that they manage the relationship between court/board and offender. Agents make decisions neither for the offender nor for the court/board. If agents look at their position from the perspective of a facilitator, they can avoid some of the pitfalls inherent in this dual role. Adopting a middle-of-the-road stance provides the best balance between being an effective advocate for the court/board and encouraging the offender to make positive changes.

## Explain the Dual Role

Agents should be up front with offenders about conditions, incentives, and sanctions. They should also be honest with the offender about their dual role as representatives of and advocates for both the offender and the supervising court/board. For instance:

> **Agent:** I want to make you aware that I have a couple of roles here. One of them is to be the agency's representative and to report on your progress on the conditions that have been set. At the same time, I act as a representative for you, to help keep the system off your back and manage

CHAPTER 6

these conditions, while possibly making some other positive steps along the way. I'll act as a "go-between"—that is, between you and the system—but ultimately you're the one who makes the choices. Tell me how that sounds to you right now. Is there anything you think I need to know before proceeding?

## Be Clear About the Sanctions

Agents should make sure offenders are aware of what sanctions are likely to occur as a result of a violation. This is perhaps most evident when the offender is getting close to receiving a sanction. In this example, the offender has shown a significant lack of progress.

> **Agent:** We've been talking this meeting about getting you up to speed on employment. We've been working together for 6 months on this, but it looks like things have been difficult for you. What happens at this point is that if you can't produce verification of employment by our next meeting, we will then move to weekly reporting. That means that instead of meeting once a month, we would meet every week. I know that would obviously make things more difficult for you, so I guess the ball's in your court. You'll have to decide whether it's easier to make time to do this or whether it's easier to take the sanction. What do you want to do about this?

Informing offenders of the sanctions can make compliance more likely, but it is by no means a magic bullet. When delivered, sanctions should be clear, immediate, and proportional to the violation. When systems adopt a progressive sanctions model, the incentives and penalties become apparent to both agents and offenders. An agent should work to ensure that an offender is never surprised by a sanction.

## Address Behavior With an "Even Keel" Attitude

Bluster, especially when addressing violations, tends to make difficult situations worse. An offender may already be on the defensive about his lack of progress, and an agitated agent can make the offender's attitude worse. For this reason, approach violations with an "even keel" attitude, addressing the behavior and dispensing the appropriate sanction, but not getting agitated or taking the violation personally. This section provides two examples of an even-keel attitude. Chapter 7 provides another example in which a violation of supervision conditions has led to revocation of the offender's probation.

The following dialogue presents a situation in which an offender is getting close to a violation of supervision orders. The agent informs him what will happen as a result of the violation, but does not get upset by the offender's attitude.

> **Agent:** We've talked about this before. In another 2 weeks, you will be in violation of this order. We have also talked about how it is up to you. You can certainly ignore this order but sanctions will be assessed.

**Offender:** Darn right, I can ignore it—this is so stupid!

**A:** It seems unfair that you're required to complete this condition. It feels like it might be a waste of your time.

**O:** Yeah, I can't believe I have to do this!

**A:** Even though it's hard to swallow, I want to make you aware of what will happen if you don't complete this. If it's not done in the next 2 weeks, you will have to start reporting to me weekly instead of monthly. I guess you have to decide whether it's easier to do it even though it seems like it might be a waste of your time, or whether it's just easier report to me more often.

**O:** You don't have to report this.

**A:** Unfortunately, that's part of my job.

**O:** You mean you can't just let it go?

**A:** No, I don't have a choice. But you have a choice, even if I don't. I'm wondering what we can do to help you succeed here?

**O:** I'll think about it; it just seems unfair.

In this example, the agent refuses to leave the middle, neither defending the order nor siding with the offender to stop the sanction. A confrontational approach is an option, but at this point, it is probably more appropriate simply to recognize the offender's reluctance and tell him what is likely to happen. Regarding the specific sanction, the agent defers to the system and emphasizes the collaborative relationship between the agent and the offender: "How do we (you, significant others, and I) keep them (the judge, the board, the agency) off your back?" This neutral stance improves the likelihood that a positive decision will eventually overtake the emotions of the moment. Finally, the agent emphasizes the offender's personal responsibility. A probationer on supervision does not have to complete the supervision conditions; he always has the option of taking the sanction.

The following dialogue illustrates another difficult situation—a positive urinalysis (UA) when the probationer denies use. In this example, the agent presents the results, refuses to defend the lab results, and immediately emphasizes the probationer's personal responsibility.

**Agent:** We got the results of your last UA and it came up positive for cocaine. Tell me what happened.

**Offender:** Positive? Are you sure? It must have been from that last use . . . what was it . . . 3 months ago?

**A:** Sort of a mystery as to how it came up dirty.

**O:** Yeah, I haven't used, so your lab must have made a mistake.

**A:** Unfortunately, the system goes strictly off the results of the UA, so there's nothing we can do about that, but you do have a couple of options at this point. It looks like there will be some jail time, but you also have the option of signing a voluntary admittance. It's a good-faith gesture, and sometimes they will go a little more leniently if they feel that the person is taking this seriously. It might mean that you could do some sort of drug treatment in lieu of jail time. On the other hand, if you decide that's not something you want, the decision will be based on the results of the UA, which will probably mean serving time in jail. But again, it's up to you.

The agent bases his or her decision on the physical evidence, rather than on the offender's admission or refusal to admit to the drug use. A dirty UA is a dirty UA. This is also the approach to take when offenders exhibit "pseudocompliance"—talking about change but showing a significant lack of progress. Agents can provide opportunities for offenders to talk and think about change, but they judge the offender's progress whether or not the offender meets the conditions of supervision.

Adopting a new approach like motivational interviewing is clearly a process. Even after initial training, many officers tend to abandon a motivational style when violations occur. If the offender shows lack of progress, a common mistake is to switch to more demanding strategies to relieve the agent's frustration. However, enforcing sanctions based on lack of progress does not mean switching to a more heavy-handed style. An agent can enforce orders and assess sanctions without leaving motivational strategies behind.

The goal is to avoid both the hard and soft approaches. The hard approach is overly directive, defending the court's/board's authority ("Don't blame the court; you're the one who broke the law."). Less examined is the "soft" approach when an officer refuses to bring violations to the court's/board's attention to save the relationship ("I won't tell this time—but don't do it again"). A positive alliance with the offender is not the same as ignoring violations. Agents can collaborate with the offender while still being true to their agency roles. They can respect personal choice yet disapprove of the behavior.

### When the Offender Denies the Initial Offense

Another difficult situation can occur when the offender denies committing the initial offense. This differs from the case when an offender denies a violation of supervision conditions in that he claims the charge was wrong from the beginning and hence he has no need to change. In working with this kind of person, some agents assume that no progress can be made unless the offender first admits the offense. Sex offenses sometimes require the offender to meet a number of supervision conditions for which admission of guilt seems to be a prerequisite—including registry, participation in a treatment group, polygraph testing, and letters expressing remorse.

As discussed earlier in this chapter, the first strategy is to avoid defending the court/board, the police report, or the test results. If the agent sees his or her role as less an interrogator and more a facilitator of certain behaviors, a middle way appears. Agents work with an offender given the conditions of supervision. The system expects certain behaviors if the offender wants to complete supervision successfully. Thus, in interacting with offenders, agents should concentrate on the observable conditions of supervision without debating the validity of the charge. Agents emphasize responsibility for future actions; the offender always has the option of taking the sanction. (Of course, it may be that the denial of the offense is accurate. The agent does not know, and so has to take the facts as presented.) Although it is best that the offender take responsibility for his past actions, admission of guilt need not always be a prerequisite of a change-focused conversation.

> **Agent:** So, because it was your car, even though you didn't know your friend stashed it under the seat, you pled "no contest" because you didn't think you could beat it, and it would cost you a lot to go to trial. So now, you're stuck with a year's supervision and all of these conditions and that's pretty frustrating to you.
>
> **Offender:** Couldn't you just put me on write-in or something?
>
> **A:** I'd be glad to work with you on that. To do that, we first need something like 6 months of good progress, so it's just a matter of navigating these first 6 months. It depends on you.
>
> **O:** But why do I have to do all these things when I'm not guilty? It's going to take a lot of time I don't have, and this substance abuse class is a joke. Sure, I've used a little weed in the past, but it's never been a problem.
>
> **A:** Kind of a rough spot to be in. Since neither of us has any control over that, what can I do to help you through the process?

The agent does not allow himself or herself to be drawn into an argument. By listening and emphasizing the offender's personal responsibility, the agent works with the offender without taking sides on the issue of innocence or guilt.

## KEY POINTS

- A person may lie to protect himself or herself or a loved one, or to protect against a perceived loss of resources.

- A respondent will bend information according to who is asking the question and how the question is phrased.

- Agents who form positive, collaborative alliances are less likely to be lied to.

- Agents should be up front with offenders as someone who represents both the offender and the criminal justice system.

- Informing offenders of the sanctions for failure to meet supervision conditions can make compliance more likely. When an offender is surprised by a sanction, this creates more resistance and less motivation to change.

- Agents should approach violations with a neutral attitude, addressing the behavior, but not taking the violation personally.

- Agents should focus on observable behavior change without being caught up in debates about innocence or guilt.

# CHAPTER 7

# From Start to Finish: Putting Motivational Interviewing Into Practice

Chapters 4, 5, and 6 presented some of the details of motivational interviewing (MI). This chapter talks about ways to put MI skills into practice. The first part covers how to apply MI to three motivational targets: importance, confidence, and commitment. The second part talks about ways to use MI in different kinds of interactions: those near the beginning (assessment and planning stage), middle (progress stage), and end (completion stage) of supervision.

## Moving From Motivation to Commitment

Chapter 2 introduced the Stages of Change model as a way to think about how people change. People who are in the early stages are low in motivation, so the task is to explore ambivalence and build motivation for change. The agent uses open-ended questions, affirmations, reflections, and summaries (OARS) to encourage talk about desire, ability, reasons, and need. At some point, the agent hopes the motivational balance will tip, and the offender will decide to make a commitment to change (DARN–C).

In the following dialogue, an agent is working with a domestic violence offender to motivate him to complete an anger management class. To structure the conversation, the agent uses the importance and confidence rulers discussed in chapter 5 and finishes with an action question.

The offender begins by defending his choices and implying that change is unnecessary. The agent ignores this less productive talk and keeps the conversation focused on change. The agent spends little time asking for details about the circumstances of the offense. In some instances, it might be helpful to understand the person's point of view, but because this offender is too angry to give a valid account of the incident, probing would probably yield little useful information. The agent acknowledges the offender's reluctance to change, but does not reinforce it. The agent uses open-ended questions, affirmations, and reflections to emphasize those parts of the offender's speech that support his motivation to change. When the offender makes

CHAPTER 7

statements about wanting to change, the agent asks an action question to steer the conversation to commitment talk. The use of importance and confidence rulers helps the offender progress from importance to confidence and finally to commitment.

**Agent:** So, one of your supervision conditions is to attend anger management classes. *[Choice of focus.]*

**Offender:** Yeah, well, my wife should be in jail for provoking me into things.

**A:** It seems to you like she shares some of the blame. *[Reflection of ambivalence.]*

**O:** And the stupid judge blew up at me for no reason. It made me so mad, when he doesn't know what really happened.

**A:** I'm glad you were able to control your temper with the judge. It shows that you are really trying. *[Affirmation.]*

**O:** If I had done what I felt like doing, he would have thrown me in jail.

**A:** So, it sounds like you have the ability to control your behavior even when you are provoked. *[Reflection.]*

**O:** Oh, I can control it when I have to. Or want to.

**A:** And with your wife, you . . . ? (Pause) *[Open-ended question.]*

**O:** To be honest with you, she just makes me so mad. Why should I be the one who always has to remain calm?

**A:** Still, with your wife's behavior, part of you wishes you had acted differently. *[Reflection of desire.]*

**O:** (Pause) I guess that's true. Like, right now, I am still so mad at her because she got me into all of this, but I guess it wasn't the best decision to slap her.

**A:** It's like part of you is still angry with her but the other part feels bad for hitting her. *[Reflection of ambivalence.]*

**O:** I guess so.

**A:** There's a part of you that wishes you could handle her behavior without losing control of your own. *[Reflection of desire.]*

**O:** (Thinking) That's right. It sounds like I don't love her, but I do. She already told the attorney that she was sorry she called the cops on me. I could tell she was sorry in court and that's why I just pled guilty. If she testified, she probably would have lied for me and I didn't want that.

The reason I was so mad when I came in here is because the D.A. was making me out to be some kind of monster and the judge went out of his way to humiliate me in front of all of those people.

A: The whole process has been bad for you. It's embarrassing to be on supervision. And now you are thinking that in spite of her behavior last night, that your love for your wife is stronger than your anger toward her. *[Reflection of reasons and desire.]*

O: Yeah.

A: There's a lot of regret there. *[Reflection of reasons.]*

O: Yeah.

A: What else has it cost you? *[Open-ended question about reasons.]*

O: (Pause) My kids. We told them to go upstairs, but they know what's going on. My parents fought like this, and it's the scariest thing you can imagine.

A: And you don't want your kids to have to go through what you went through. *[Reflection of desire.]*

O: (Thinking) And it's self-respect. It's not just my wife, but the people I know, my friends and coworkers—I would die if they knew what happened.

A: So, let me see if I've got this right: You and your wife were having a verbal altercation where you got so angry, you hit her. She called the cops. Even though you are still a little angry with her, part of you knows that your behavior was wrong. And now, you wish you had a way of behaving better in this situation. So, where does that leave you? *[Summary, open-ended question about commitment.]*

O: Well, I wish we both knew a better way of handling things.

A: Let me ask you this. How important is it to you to have a better way—let's say on a scale of 1 to 10, with 1 being not important and 10 being very important—how important is it to you that you handle future conflicts with your wife better? *[Open-ended question about desire.]*

O: Definitely, a 10.

A: It's at the very top. Why a 10 and not a lower number? *[Reflection of desire, open-ended question.]*

O: Well, I want us to be happy and to be there for each other. I hate all of this.

**A:** So, changing this behavior couldn't be more important. *[Reflection of desire.]*

**O:** That's right.

**A:** On the same scale, how confident are you that you could change your behavior if you wanted to? *[Open-ended question about ability.]*

**O:** Right now, I want to say a 10, but I don't really know. Maybe about a 5.

**A:** You're pretty confident. *[Reflection of ability.]*

**O:** Yeah, there's a couple of things I can do.

**A:** What would it take to get that number up a little, say to a 6 or 7? *[Open-ended question.]*

**O:** (Thinking) I don't know. I'm just not sure just these anger management classes will help. I think we both should get some counseling or something. I know we are going to forgive each other when I get home, but, tomorrow, all of the same problems—the bills, the kids, time for ourselves—it's all still going to be there.

**A:** So, maybe getting some help for the both of you would bring that to a 6 or 7. *[Reflection of commitment.]*

**O:** We can't afford it. Our financial situation is one of the biggest stresses.

**A:** So, if there were a place that took into consideration your financial situation, you would be more willing to go there. *[Reflection of commitment.]*

**O:** Oh, I would definitely go. I think my wife would too, since she has brought it up before.

**A:** So, what would you like to do about that? *[Action question about commitment.]*

## Adapting Motivational Interviewing to Different Kinds of Interviews

This section talks about using MI during three stages of the supervision process: near (or before) the start of the term of supervision, in the middle of the term of supervision, and closer to discharge or revocation.

### The First Meeting

An offender may already have formed a number of impressions even before the first interview with his probation or parole officer. He may have been ordered to appear at the probation or parole office at an inconvenient time, had his fingernail clippers confiscated at security, seen a host of signs prohibiting some things and ordering others, and had to wait in a cold, unfriendly waiting room. Given these conditions, an agent can gain or lose influence by how he or she greets the offender.

Early meetings lay the foundation for how offenders and agents will interact in later meetings. In departments with separate intake staff, the intake interview heavily influences the ease or difficulty of the initial meeting between the offender and the agent. In fact, some officers say that they can predict whether an offender will show up for his initial appointment based on which intake officer he sees. One officer reports, "If I see one name, I know the person will be reluctant to come in and I'll spend a portion of my time trying to undo all the damage that the intake officer caused. If I see the other name, not only do I know the client will show, I know I will have a hard time living up to the positive image that this officer created. It's like night and day."

Discussing the conditions of supervision is the first task in most initial meetings. Even though it is routine for the agent, it may be intimidating and overwhelming for the offender. One way to address this anxiety is to spend a moment talking about how the person feels about being on supervision:

> **Agent:** Mr. Campbell, I see you've been placed on probation for theft. As you are aware, there are a number of conditions that we'll have to cover. But I'm wondering if we can spend a minute talking about what it's like for you to be on supervision.

The conversation might also touch on how the person feels about the activities that have caused him to be on supervision:

> **Agent:** I have the police report and know something about why you're on supervision, but I'm more interested in hearing how you see things. From your perspective, what happened to bring you here?

Other agents use the initial conversations to talk about the offender's key values, interests, or significant relationships. These moments are a way to gather information and set the tone for subsequent meetings. The following exchange shows how one agent handles the first few seconds of an early routine interview:

> **Agent:** Hi Mark, thanks for coming in. How are you?
>
> **Offender:** Pretty good.
>
> **A:** How was your weekend?
>
> **O:** It was okay. Pretty busy with all the overtime.
>
> **A:** How's the family? I think your daughter was sick the last time we talked.

## CHAPTER 7

**O:** Oh yeah, it was no big deal. We did have to spend last Saturday in the ER, but it turned out to be just a cold.

**A:** Boy, those ER visits can be brutal. You sit there for hours with a sick kid, not knowing when they will see you. I'm glad she's all right. So anyway, let me explain what I want to do today. I have a few questions about how things are going with your supervision up to this point, and I'd also like to hear about any concerns you have that I might be able to assist you with so that we can keep you in compliance with your conditions. So what's been going on that might affect your supervision?

The agent spends the first 30 seconds of the interview chatting with the offender and then moves to the business at hand. Rather than having a stern or prepackaged attitude, this agent is honest, empathetic, and collaborative. Notice also that the agent remembers and asks about an issue the offender mentioned during their previous meeting. This inquiry shows that the agent is interested enough to remember something that is important to the offender.

### Motivational Interviewing and the Case-Planning Interview

Case management helps connect assessment, planning, and supervision. This section talks about ways to use assessment results to guide the case-planning process.

There are four basic steps to case planning:

1. Consult the assessment results for information on risk, needs, and responsivity.
2. Ask the offender what problem(s) he thinks are most closely related to his crime.
3. Factor in any relevant court- or board-ordered conditions.
4. Given the information from all three areas, use MI strategies to help resolve ambivalence and motivate positive behavior.

In the following interview, the agent uses the results of a risk/needs assessment to initiate a conversation about change. The agent presents the results of the assessment and discusses the first of three dynamic risk factors. Because the offender seems committed to action but has only a vague plan, the agent asks permission to assist him in developing a more specific plan. At this point, the agent might continue to focus on anger management or proceed to another issue that puts the offender at risk of committing another crime or otherwise violating the conditions of supervision.

**Agent:** Last time we talked, I asked you some questions about areas that might place you at risk. I'd like to explain a little about the results. *[Request for permission.]*

**Offender:** Sure.

**A:** OK, let's look this over together. Over here is a risk scale. It indicates that you are at the high end of medium risk. According to the scale, the factors that put you there are that you have been in trouble before, that most of your friends have been in trouble before, and that you have had some problems in the past managing your anger. What do you think? *[Information, open-ended question.]*

**O:** Well, I know I'm not going to get in trouble again—I'm sure of it.

**A:** Great. You're really confident. *[Affirmation, reflection.]*

**O:** I am.

**A:** Good. Maybe we can talk about some things you'd be willing to do right now to reduce your risk. *[Information.]*

**O:** Well, I have already decided not to do stuff without thinking about it. My brother Jake is already doing time for this, so I won't be hanging out with him. And I know I told you I used to blow up and stuff, but I'm not going to do that any more.

**A:** Good for you. It's important to you to look at some of these behaviors because you don't want this kind of trouble again. Tell me a little about how you decided this. *[Affirmation, reflection, open-ended question.]*

**O:** Well, for one thing, Jake's in jail. Then my girlfriend broke up with me for a couple of months, and I lost a lot of time at work because of all of this. All of my vacation and sick time are used up, and I've got all of the court costs to pay.

**A:** I remember you saying that your anger and some of your friends were factors in the last two offenses. *[Reflection.]*

**O:** Yeah, I'll just have to watch those things this time. I'll stay away from those people that get me worked up.

**A:** Good for you. You already have some ideas about ways to manage your anger. *[Affirmation, reflection.]*

**O:** Well, I just know I have to.

**A:** Tell me about a time when you got angry but were able to calm yourself down. How did you manage those angry feelings? *[Open-ended question.]*

**O:** (Pause) Well, that counting to 10 stuff doesn't work. I can tell you that. (Pause)

**A:** OK, it's helpful to be aware of things that don't work for you. But I'm wondering what does work for you. *[Open-ended question.]*

**O:** I don't know. I guess I just don't get angry.

**A:** I wonder if you'd be interested in some suggestions about maybe getting some help in this area. *[Request for permission.]*

**O:** Do you mean a headshrinker? I can't afford that.

**A:** That may be one solution, but there are also other options. We have some classes here where regular guys like you learn some ways of dealing better with their anger. Or, we have some counselors—not headshrinkers, but just ordinary counselors that talk to people one on one. I could also refer you to a counselor not connected to our agency, or you may have other things you've thought of. *[Menu of options.]*

**O:** Are any of them free?

**A:** Not quite, but the group meetings are the lowest priced. *[Information.]*

**O:** Could I just try it out and if it doesn't help me try something else?

**A:** Sure. You want a program that really helps you. *[Reflection.]*

**O:** Yeah, when would I have to start and how often would I have to go? What are they like?

**A:** (Provides information about the classes.) So, I'm wondering what you'd like to get out of the class. How would you like things to be different when you finish? *[Information, open-ended question.]*

## Motivational Interviewing and Routine Meetings

As the offender moves through the supervision process, the agent might be tempted to relax and concentrate his or her attention elsewhere. The agent expects that the meetings will become shorter and more routine. However, it is important for the agent to stay alert to the offender's change process. The action stage may be marked by awkward attempts, difficult situations, and slips. Thus, some of the major tasks for meetings during the middle of the supervision process include encouraging and reinforcing progress, solving problems, and preventing relapses.

Agents not only work with offenders to change their behavior but must also document compliance with the conditions of supervision. This is a lot to manage in a short amount of time. Fortunately, the two tasks frequently overlap. For instance, a condition to pay fees may overlap with the agent's desire to increase the offender's motivation to get a job. The tasks are logically connected and both involve behavior change. True, the case plan is more about long-term changes in behavior and seeks the offender's input, whereas conditions are usually more short-term and dictated by the court or board. Nevertheless, because both seek to change behavior, the skills and techniques of MI are relevant in both instances.

Two documents guide the interview process: the case plan and the conditions of supervision. To structure an interview, some agents prefer to address compliance first, others prefer to address the case plan first, and still others allow the offender to choose. The following dialogue presents a routine interview from start to finish. The agent begins with a few casual comments and then allows the offender to decide which issue they will cover first. The agent uses open-ended questions and reflections to gather information and document compliance with the conditions of supervision. The agent also asks questions about and encourages the offender to use class material. The interview ends with other documentation questions, a summary, and an affirmation.

> **Agent:** Mr. Peterson, thanks for coming in today. I know you had some difficulty with the original time. *[Greeting.]*
>
> **Offender:** Well, you being willing to change the appointment time really helped a lot.
>
> **A:** Good, I'm glad it helped. Things do sometimes come up, and I appreciate you letting me know in advance. Go ahead, have a chair. (Both take seats.) So how have you been? *[Affirmation, open-ended question.]*
>
> **O:** Oh, pretty good, mostly.
>
> **A:** Good, glad to hear that. Well, as usual, I want to check in today and see how things are going with your supervision. So how are things progressing? *[Setting agenda, open-ended question.]*
>
> **O:** I'm halfway done with my community service. I'm putting in 8 hours a week at the homeless shelter. I brought in a payment for restitution and costs. I'm up to date on both of those things. And I've been going to my anger management classes. As far as I know I'm doing everything I am supposed to.
>
> **A:** Good. You're making your supervision a priority. *[Affirmation, reflection.]*
>
> **O:** Yeah, and that's not easy. You know money is tight, and my wife really gets on me about having to pay $120 a month that we really could use for other things. But I think if it wasn't for my anger management classes, I may have blown up again and done something stupid, so maybe they are doing me some good. I was able to use OPV this week to help me not blow up at her.
>
> **A:** OPV? *[Open-ended question.]*
>
> **O:** You don't know what OPV is?
>
> **A:** Tell me about it. *[Open-ended question.]*

**O:** It stands for "other people's point of view." It means we've got to listen to other people and try to see things from their point of view.

**A:** Good principle. So, how do you use that when your wife gets on you about the money? *[Affirmation, open-ended question.]*

**O:** Well, part of it is a thinking thing. I have to think to myself, "Why is she doing this?" Then I think, "Well, it isn't her fault I got in that argument and busted out the guy's windshield." So I guess seeing it from her point of view helps calm me down a little.

**A:** Wow, it's nice to see that it's paying off for you. Even though you had mixed feelings about going, you're using it to your advantage. Let me also ask you a question about fees. You said you are up to date on your payments, but my records show you are $150 in arrears. *[Affirmation, reflection, open-ended question, second agenda item.]*

**O:** Well, I'm up to date on my restitution and fees. On my money order, I always put, "for supervision fees and restitution only," because I am not making payments on the attorney fees.

**A:** So you're behind on those. *[Reflection.]*

**O:** Well, I've been practicing in my class for this. I really think that the court tricked me on attorney fees.

**A:** Tricked you? *[Open-ended question.]*

**O:** Yeah, when I went to court, we were really behind in our bills and were thinking of declaring bankruptcy. So the judge says that if I can't afford an attorney, he would appoint one. So I told him my situation and he appointed one. Well, then I found out I would probably have gotten the same sentence if I didn't have an attorney, but now I got charged $1,500 for the attorney to go in there and plead me guilty. I never even got a chance to tell my side of the story. The judge didn't tell me I was going to end up having to pay for this attorney until after I got supervision. So I don't think that's fair.

**A:** That part of the fees was a surprise to you. *[Reflection.]*

**O:** Well, yeah. I guess I should have figured it out, but still, $1,500 for paperwork? Come on!

**A:** So, at this point, it's part of your supervision, but you have mixed feelings about it. So what do you want to do about it? *[Reflection, open-ended question.]*

**O:** Well, we did this exercise in class where I decided that I would like to stand up to the judge and not pay the fees, even if I end up having to sit in jail for it.

**A:** That is your decision. But I want you to be aware that if that happens, that would be a violation and you would have to answer to the judge. *[Affirmation of choice, information.]*

**O:** Yeah, I know. But I don't know what's going to happen, because I haven't talked to my wife about this yet. Who knows, in the end I might chicken out and just pay the fees.

**A:** OK, so you are behind on the payment of the attorney fees. If you like, we can leave that discussion until the next meeting to give you a chance to talk with your wife. So, what else is going on that might affect your supervision? *[Reflection, provision of choice, open-ended question.]*

**O:** That's about all I can think of. Oh, I might need a travel permit to go to my wife's parents for Thanksgiving.

**A:** Okay, let me give you this request for travel permit form to fill out if you decide to go. What else? *[Information, open-ended question.]*

**O:** I think that's it.

**A:** Okay. As always, I need to know whether you have violated any conditions of your supervision since I last saw you. *[Closed question.]*

**O:** Nope.

**A:** And the last thing is the verification of your community service hours from the homeless shelter. *[Closed question.]*

**O:** Oh, yeah, here it is.

**A:** It sounds like things are going reasonably well for you. You've been using the material from the classes and really working hard to manage that anger and stay out of trouble. You've been diligent about most of your obligations, which you plan on continuing, but you're not sure yet what you want to do about the attorney fees. Did I miss anything? How about I see you 2 weeks from today at the same time? *[Summary, affirmation.]*

**O:** Yeah, that's fine.

**A:** What you're doing in your class is pretty interesting. I look forward to the next meeting. *[Affirmation.]*

**O:** Sure. See you in 2 weeks.

## Motivational Interviewing and the Postviolation Interview

Based on its track record, MI can be expected to reduce violations. However, it is certainly not a panacea; it only increases the probability of change. Supervision orders are sometimes given with an idealized expectation of behavior. The court or board expects the offender to comply with all conditions without any failures or setbacks, but for most people, slips are a normal part of the change process. This more realistic view of change allows agents to take violations in stride. Agents can address lapses and violations without leaving a motivational style.

Chapter 6 gave two examples of ways to maintain this even-keel attitude when addressing different violations. The next dialogue provides an additional example, in which a serious violation has placed the offender in jail. This postviolation interview focuses on providing information, while leaving the door open to future interactions. This agent demonstrates most of the style measures of MI, including empathy, acceptance, and support for autonomy. The agent's goal is to provide information while not taking sides on the issue of guilt or innocence. In this instance, values are irrelevant; the focus is, and must be, on the here and now.

> **Agent:** Hello Mr. Juarez. It's disappointing to be visiting you in jail. *[Empathetic opening.]*
>
> **Offender:** I hope you don't believe that I did anything to that little girl.
>
> **A:** What I believe isn't really important here, so maybe I should define my role. You have been accused of a serious violation, one that requires me to file for a revocation hearing. You started by telling me that you didn't do anything, but unfortunately I'm not in a position to decide whether you did or didn't. As your probation officer, I have to take the allegations at face value. So I need to explain the revocation process to you and let you know about your due process rights. I want you to be treated fairly and I'll do what I can to make sure that happens. So, while I am explaining the procedures, if there is anything you don't understand, please let me know. On the other hand, if there are things you don't agree with, you should know that I don't have any control over these procedures at this point. It's back in the court's hands. Is that clear? *[Definition of role, maintenance of a neutral stance with regard to the facts.]*
>
> **O:** Yeah, I guess, but it doesn't seem fair. You're supposed to be innocent until proven guilty.
>
> **A:** So, you see the process as unfair, but I do want to be fair with you. *[Reflection, avoidance of argument.]*
>
> **O:** (Silence)
>
> **A:** (Explains all of the procedures one at a time and after each one asks:) What questions do you have? *[Information.]*

**O:** Are you going to testify against me?

**A:** If you contest, I will probably be called as a witness. I will give a summary of your progress using the reports I am required to file. If you do decide to contest, I'd be glad to go over it with you before the hearing so that you have a chance to correct anything in the report that you don't think is factual. If we end up disagreeing about anything, you can point that out to your attorney and he can cross-examine me about those things. *[Information.]*

**O:** Can't you help me?

**A:** Unfortunately, there's nothing I can do at this point. I can say that I care about you getting your life together and I would be glad to continue to work with you if the court allows you to continue your supervision. *[Indication of concern for offender's welfare, information.]*

**O:** So, you're not hoping I go down?

**A:** Mr. Juarez, I don't know whether you did or didn't commit the violation because I wasn't there. I do wish that things had turned out differently for you, but I'm not the one to judge you on the violation. *[Maintenance of a neutral stance.]*

**O:** Thanks, I guess.

**A:** I'll check with you before your revocation hearing starts if you decide to contest. What other questions do you have for me right now? *[Indication of concern for offender's welfare, open-ended question.]*

## Managing Time Constraints

High caseloads and limited resources are real problems in corrections. For years, agents have had to do more and more with less and less. Thus, MI may seem like another imposition on the already limited time that agents have—one more thing to add to the already considerable demands of the job. Certainly, learning MI strategies requires an investment of time. However, if MI delivers on its promises, this investment has a payoff. MI does not require performing new tasks, but rather adopting a new set of strategies for performing old tasks more effectively and efficiently.

Time management requires an additional set of strategies that are beyond the scope of this guide. Effective agents use MI principles to guide their interactions and are efficient in conducting interviews. An efficient interview involves—

1. Setting the agenda at the start.
2. Covering topics one at a time.

# CHAPTER 7

3. Keeping the interview progressing in a linear fashion without moving backward or jumping from topic to topic.

4. Ending with a summary of what was discussed, what the offender agrees to do (or what the penalty will be for noncompliance), and the offender's most important reasons for action.

Along the way, effective agents tailor their interactions based on the stage of change. If the offender is ambivalent, the agent uses strategies that target motivation for change. On the other hand, if the offender is ready to take action, an effective agent moves toward action-oriented strategies and only occasionally revisits motivation.

Careful listening takes time, but the effective interviewer saves time by more efficiently steering the conversation toward change. The offender becomes less defensive and more cooperative. The motivationally inclined agent does not spend time debating conditions, arguing, or threatening. This active role relieves the agent of the ultimate responsibility for solving the offender's problems; the offender becomes responsible for his own actions. Finally, as the offender improves his behavior and compliance with the conditions of his supervision, the agent can expect to spend less time on investigations, documenting violations, and writing revocation reports. Offenders who are well prepared for change require less supervision time and use fewer scarce resources. People who are changing for the better are likely to see improvements in their lives, the lives of their families, and lives of their communities.

## KEY POINTS

- Consider structuring a conversation using the importance and confidence rulers and questions discussed in chapter 5.

- Use open-ended questions, affirmations, reflections, and summaries (OARS) to gather information and keep the conversation focused on change.

- Use the first few minutes of an interaction to build rapport with the offender and lay the foundation for what comes later.

- Focus on mandated conditions and other areas of positive behavior change. Consider using the results of a risk/needs assessment to initiate a conversation about specific areas of change.

- Address lapses and violations without leaving a motivational style. Leave the door open to subsequent interactions.

# REFERENCES

Amrhein, P.C., Miller, W.R., Yahne, C.E., Palmer, M., and Fulcher, L. 2003. Client commitment language during motivational interviewing predicts drug use outcomes. *Journal of Consulting and Clinical Psychology* 71(5): 862–878.

Andrews, D.A., and Bonta, J. 2003. *The Psychology of Criminal Conduct,* 3d ed. Cincinnati: Anderson Publishing Co.

Andrews, D.A., Zinger, I., Hoge, R.D., Bonta, J., Gendreau, P., and Cullen, F.T. 1990. Does correctional treatment work? A clinically relevant and psychologically informed meta-analysis. *Criminology* 28(3): 369–404.

Baker, A., Lewin, T., Reichler, H., Clancy, R., Carr, V., Garrett, R., Sly, K., Devir, H., and Terry, M. 2002. Evaluation of a motivational interview for substance use within psychiatric in-patient services. *Addiction* 97(10): 1329–1337.

Bem, D.J. 1972. Self-perception theory. In L. Berkowitz (ed.), *Advances in Experimental Social Psychology,* vol. 6, pp. 1–62. New York: Academic Press.

Berg, I.K. 1994. *Family Based Services: A Solution-Focused Approach.* New York: Norton.

Berk, M., Berk, L., and Castle, D. 2004. A collaborative approach to the treatment alliance in bipolar disorder. *Bipolar Disorders* 6(6): 504–518.

Bien, T.H., Miller, W.R., and Boroughs, J.M. 1993. Motivational interviewing with alcohol outpatients. *Behavioural and Cognitive Psychotherapy* 21(4): 347–356.

Brecht, M.L., Anglin, M.D., and Jung-Chi, W. 1993. Treatment effectiveness for legally coerced versus voluntary methadone maintenance clients. *American Journal of Drug and Alcohol Abuse* 19(1): 89–107.

Brown, J.M., and Miller, W.R. 1993. Impact of motivational interviewing on participation and outcome in residential alcoholism treatment. *Psychology of Addictive Behaviors* 7: 211–218.

Carnegie, D. 1998. *How to Win Friends and Influence People.* New York: Pocket Books.

# REFERENCES

Clark, M., Walters, S.T., Gingerich, R., and Meltzer, M. 2006. Motivational interviewing for probation officers: Tipping the balance towards change. *Federal Probation* 70(1): 38–44.

Clark, M.D. 1998. Strength-based practice: The ABC's of working with adolescents who don't want to work with you. *Federal Probation* 62(1): 46–53.

Clark, M.D. 2006. Entering the business of behavior change: Motivational interviewing for probation staff. *Perspectives* 30(1): 38–45.

Cullen, F.T. 2002. Rehabilitation and treatment programs. In J.Q. Wilson and J. Petersilia (eds.), *Crime: Public Policy for Crime Control,* 2d ed., pp. 253–289. Oakland, CA: ICS Press.

Cullen, F.T., and Gendreau, P. 2000. Assessing correctional rehabilitation: Policy, practice, and prospects. In J. Horney (ed.), *Criminal Justice 2000, Volume 3: Policies, Processes, and Decisions of the Criminal Justice System,* pp. 109–175. Washington, DC: U.S. Department of Justice, Office of Justice Programs, National Institute of Justice. NCJ 182410.

Cullen, F.T, and Gendreau, P. 2001. From nothing works to what works: Changing professional ideology in the 21st century. *Prison Journal* 81(3): 313–338.

Daley, D.C., Salloum, I.M., Zuckoff, A., Kirisci, L., and Thase, M.E. 1998. Increasing treatment adherence among outpatients with depression and cocaine dependence: Results of a pilot study. *The American Journal of Psychiatry* 155(11): 1611–1613.

Deci, E.L., and Ryan, R.M. 1985. *Intrinsic Motivation and Self-Determination in Human Behavior.* New York: Plenum.

DiClemente, C.C., Bellino, L.E., and Neavins, T.M. 1999. Motivation for change and alcoholism treatment. *Alcohol Research and Health* 23(2): 86–92.

Dunn, C., Droesch, R.M., Johnston, B.D., and Rivara, F.P. 2004. Motivational interviewing with injured adolescents in the emergency department: In-session predictors of change. *Behavioural and Cognitive Psychotherapy* 32(1): 113–116.

Easton, C., Swan, S., and Sinha, R. 2000. Motivation to change substance use among offenders of domestic violence. *Journal of Substance Abuse Treatment* 19(1): 1–5.

Erickson, S.J., Gerstle, M., and Feldstein, S.W. 2005. Brief interventions and motivational interviewing with children, adolescents, and their parents in pediatric health care settings: A review. *Archives of Pediatrics and Adolescent Medicine* 159(12): 1173–1180.

# REFERENCES

Farbring, C.A. 2002. Short reflections on Affirm: The least emphasized method in MI. *Motivational Interviewing Newsletter: Updates, Education and Training* 9(2): 4–6.

Gendreau, P., Goggin, C., Cullen, F., and Paparozzi, M. 2002. The common-sense revolution and correctional policy. In J. McGuire (ed.), *Offender Rehabilitation and Treatment: Effective Programmes and Policies To Reduce Re-offending,* pp. 359–386. Chichester, England: John Wiley and Sons.

Gendreau, P., Little, T., and Goggin, C. 1996. A meta-analysis of the predictors of adult offender rehabilitation: What works. *Criminology* 34(4): 575–608.

Gibbs, J.P. 1986. Deterrence theory and research. In G.B. Melton (ed.), *The Law as a Behavioral Instrument: Nebraska Symposium on Motivation,* vol. 33, pp. 87–130. Lincoln, NE: University of Nebraska Press.

Ginsburg, J.I.D., Mann, R.E., Rotgers, F., and Weekes, J.R. 2002. Motivational interviewing with criminal justice populations. In W.R. Miller and S. Rollnick (eds.), *Motivational Interviewing: Preparing People To Change,* 2d ed., pp. 333–346. New York: Guilford Press.

Harper, R., and Hardy, S. 2000. An evaluation of motivational interviewing as a method of intervention with clients in a probation setting. *British Journal of Social Work* 30(3): 393–400.

Hettema, J., Steele, J., and Miller, W.R. 2005. Motivational interviewing. *Annual Review of Clinical Psychology* 1(1): 91–111.

Hollin, C. 2001. To treat or not to treat? An historical perspective. In C. Hollin (ed.), *Handbook of Offender Assessment and Treatment,* pp. 3–15. Chichester, England: John Wiley and Sons.

Hubble, M., Duncan, B., and Miller, S. 1999. *The Heart and Soul of Change: What Works in Therapy.* Washington, DC: American Psychological Association.

Kear-Colwell, J., and Pollock, P. 1997. Motivation or confrontation. Which approach to the child sex offender? *Criminal Justice and Behavior* 24(1): 20–33.

Lanceley, F.J. 2003. *On-Scene Guide for Crisis Negotiators,* 2d ed. Boca Raton, FL: CRC Press.

Latessa, E.J., Cullen, F.T., and Gendreau, P. 2002. Beyond correctional quackery: Professionalism and the possibility of effective treatment. *Federal Probation* 66(2): 43–49.

Lipchik, E., Becker, M., Brasher, B., Derks, J., and Volkmann, J. 2005. Neuroscience. A new direction for solution focused thinkers? *Journal of Systemic Therapies* 24(3): 49–69.

# REFERENCES

Lipton, D., Martinson, R., and Wilks, J. 1975. *The Effectiveness of Correctional Treatment: A Survey of Treatment Evaluation Strategies.* New York: Praeger.

Mann, R.E., Ginsburg, J.I.D., and Weekes, J.R. 2002. Motivational interviewing with offenders. In M. McMurran (ed.), *Motivating Offenders To Change: A Guide to Enhancing Engagement in Therapy,* pp. 87–102. West Sussex, England: John Wiley and Sons.

Mann, R.E., and Rollnick, S. 1996. Motivational interviewing with a sex offender who believed he was innocent. *Behavioural and Cognitive Psychotherapy* 24: 127–134.

Markland, D., Ryan, R.M., Tobin, V.J., and Rollnick, S. 2005. Motivational interviewing and self-determination theory. *Journal of Social and Clinical Psychology* 24(6): 811–831.

Marques, P.R., Voas, R.B., Tippetts, A.S., and Beirness, D.J. 1999. Behavioral monitoring of DUI offenders with the Alcohol Ignition Interlock Recorder. *Addiction* 94(12): 1861–1870.

Martino, S., Carroll, K., Kostas, D., Perkins, J., and Rounsaville, B. 2002. Dual diagnosis motivational interviewing: A modification of motivational interviewing for substance-abusing patients with psychotic disorders. *Journal of Substance Abuse Treatment* 23(4): 297–308.

Martino, S., Carroll, K.M., O'Malley, S.S., and Rounsaville, B.J. 2000. Motivational interviewing with psychiatrically ill substance-abusing patients. *American Journal on Addictions* 9(1): 88–91.

Martinson, R. 1974. What works? Questions and answers about prison reform. *The Public Interest* 35: 22–54.

Maruna, S., and LeBel, T. 2003. Welcome home? Examining the "Reentry Court" concept from a strengths perspective. *Western Criminology Review* 4(2): 91–107.

McGuire, J. 1995. *What Works: Reducing Reoffending—Guidelines From Research and Practice.* New York: John Wiley and Sons.

McGuire, J. 2002. Integrating findings from research reviews. In J. McGuire (ed.), *Offender Rehabilitation and Treatment: Effective Programmes and Policies To Reduce Re-Offending,* pp. 3–38. Chichester, England: John Wiley and Sons.

Miller, N.S., and Flaherty, J.A. 2000. Effectiveness of coerced addiction treatment (alternative consequences): A review of the clinical research. *Journal of Substance Abuse Treatment* 18(1): 9–16.

Miller, W.R. 1985. Motivation for treatment: A review with special emphasis on alcoholism. *Psychological Bulletin* 98(1): 84–107.

Miller, W.R., Meyers, R.J., and Tonigan, J.S. 1999. Engaging the unmotivated in treatment for alcohol problems: A comparison of three strategies for intervention through family members. *Journal of Consulting and Clinical Psychology* 67(5): 688–697.

Miller, W.R., and Rollnick, S. 2002. *Motivational Interviewing: Preparing People for Change,* 2d ed. New York: Guilford Press.

Miller, W.R., Zweben, J., and Johnson, W.R. 2005. Evidence-based treatment: Why, what, where, when, and how? *Journal of Substance Abuse Treatment* 29(4): 267–276.

Monti, P.M., Colby, S.M., Barnett, N.P., Spirito, A., Rohsenow, D.J., Myers, M., Woolard, R., and Lewander, W. 1999. Brief intervention for harm reduction with alcohol-positive older adolescents in a hospital emergency department. *Journal of Consulting and Clinical Psychology* 67(6): 989–994.

Monti, P.M., Colby, S.M., and O'Leary, T.A. 2001. *Adolescents, Alcohol, and Substance Abuse: Reaching Teens Through Brief Interventions.* New York: Guilford Press.

Moyers, T.B., and Martin, T. 2006. Therapist influence on client language during motivational interviewing sessions. *Journal of Substance Abuse Treatment* 30: 245–251.

Moyers, T.B., Miller, W.R., and Hendrickson, S.M.L. 2005. How does motivational interviewing work? Therapist interpersonal skill as a predictor of client behavior within motivational interviewing sessions. *Journal of Consulting and Clinical Psychology* 73(4): 590–598.

National Institute of Corrections. 2003. *Implementing Evidence-Based Practice in Community Corrections: The Principles of Effective Intervention.* Washington DC: U.S. Department of Justice, National Institute of Corrections. NIC Accession Number 019342.

Prochaska, J.O., DiClemente, C.C., and Norcross, J.C. 1992. In search of how people change: Applications to addictive behaviors. *American Psychologist* 47(9): 1102–1114.

Prochaska, J.O., and Levesque, D.A. 2002. Enhancing motivation of offenders at each stage of change and phase of therapy. In M. McMurran (ed.), *Motivating Offenders To Change: A Guide to Enhancing Engagement in Therapy,* pp. 57–73. West Sussex, England: John Wiley and Sons.

Project MATCH Research Group. 1997. Matching alcoholism treatments to client heterogeneity: Project MATCH posttreatment drinking outcomes. *Journal of Studies on Alcohol* 58: 7–29.

# REFERENCES

Project MATCH Research Group. 1998. Matching alcoholism treatments to client heterogeneity: Project MATCH three-year drinking outcomes. *Alcoholism, Clinical and Experimental Research* 22(6): 1300–1311.

Rapp, C. 1998. *The Strengths Model: Case Management With People Suffering From Severe and Persistent Mental Illness.* New York: Oxford University Press.

Rogers, C.R. 1961. O*n Becoming a Person: A Therapist's View of Psychotherapy.* Boston: Houghton Mifflin.

Rollnick, S. 1998. Readiness, importance, and confidence: Critical conditions of change in treatment. In W.R. Miller and N. Heather (eds.), *Treating Addictive Behaviors,* 2d ed., pp. 49–60. New York: Plenum.

Rubak, S., Sandboek, A., Lauritzen, T., and Christensen, B. 2005. Motivational interviewing: A systematic review and meta-analysis. *British Journal of General Practice* 55(513): 305–312.

Ryan, R.M., and Deci, E.L. 2000. Self-determination theory and the facilitation of intrinsic motivation, social development, and well-being. *The American Psychologist,* 55(1): 68–78.

Ryan, R.M., Plant, R.W., and O'Malley, S. 1995. Initial motivations for alcohol treatment: Relations with patient characteristics, treatment involvement, and dropout. *Addictive Behaviors* 20(3): 279–297.

Saarni, C., and Lewis, M. 1993. Deceit and illusion in human affairs. In M. Lewis and C. Saarni (eds.), *Lying and Deception in Everyday Life.* New York: Guilford Press.

Saleebey, D. (ed.). 1992. *The Strengths Perspective in Social Work Practice.* New York: Longman.

Sigmon, S., and Snyder, C.R. 1993. Looking at oneself in a rose-colored mirror: The role of excuses in the negotiation of personal reality. In M. Lewis and C. Saarni (eds.), *Lying and Deception in Everyday Life.* New York: Guilford Press.

Skinner, B.F. 1953. *Science and Human Behavior.* New York: Free Press.

Taxman, F.S. 1999. Unraveling "what works" for offenders in substance abuse treatment. *National Drug Court Institute Review* 2(2): 93–134.

Taxman, F.S., and Bouffard, J. 2000. The importance of systems in improving offender outcomes: Critical elements of treatment integrity. *Justice Research and Policy* 2(2): 9–30.

Taxman, F.S., Shepardson, E.S., and Byrne, J.M. 2004. *Tools of the Trade: A Guide to Incorporating Science Into Practice.* Washington, DC: U.S. Department of Justice, National Institute of Corrections, and Maryland Department of Public Safety and Correctional Services. NIC Accession Number 020095.

# REFERENCES

Tevyaw, T.O., and Monti, P.M. 2004. Motivational enhancement and other brief interventions for adolescent substance abuse: Foundations, applications and evaluations. *Addiction* 99: 63–75.

Toch, H. 2000. Altruistic activity as correctional treatment. *International Journal of Offender Therapy and Comparative Criminology* 44: 270–278.

Trotter, C. 1999. *Working With Involuntary Clients: A Guide to Practice.* Thousand Oaks, CA: Sage Publications.

Ury, W. 1993. *Getting Past No: Negotiating Your Way From Confrontation to Cooperation.* New York, NY: Bantam Books.

Vivian-Byrne, S. 2004. Changing people's minds. *Journal of Social Aggression* 10(2): 181–192.

Wampold, B.E., Mondin, G.W., Moody, M., Stich, F., Benson, K., and Ahn, H.N. 1997. A meta-analysis of outcome studies comparing bona fide psychotherapies: Empirically, "all must have prizes." *Psychological Bulletin* 122(3): 203–215.

Ward, T., and Brown, M. 2004. The good lives model and conceptual issues in offender rehabilitation. *Psychology Crime and Law* 10(3): 243–257.

Wild, T.C., Newton-Taylor, B., and Alletto, R. 1998. Perceived coercion among clients entering substance abuse treatment: Structural and psychological determinants. *Addictive Behaviors* 23(1): 81–95.

# ABOUT THE AUTHORS

Scott T. Walters, Ph.D., is Assistant Professor of Health Promotion and Behavioral Sciences at the University of Texas School of Public Health. He is the author of more than 30 journal articles and 4 books, including, most recently, *Talking with College Students about Alcohol: Motivational Strategies for Reducing Abuse* (Guilford Press, 2006). Using the evidence-based approach of motivational interviewing, Dr. Walters has trained providers to implement behavior change strategies in medical, counseling, social work, and criminal justice contexts. Dr. Walters has received national and international awards for his efforts to bridge research and practice, including the 2006 University of Cincinnati Award from the American Probation and Parole Association. Web site: *http://myprofile.cos.com/swalters*.

Michael D. Clark, M.S.W., L.M.S.W., is a consultant, trainer, and addictions therapist. After 18 years of direct practice as a probation officer and court magistrate, he is currently director of the Center for Strength-Based Strategies in Michigan. This organization emphasizes skill building for direct practice and building the capacity for strength-based and motivational approaches within justice organizations. With more than 25 articles and book chapters to his credit, Mr. Clark specializes in training probation and parole staff and has presented to groups throughout the United States and in Europe, Canada, the Caribbean, and the Pacific rim. Web site: *http://www.buildmotivation.com*.

Ray Gingerich is semiretired from 35 years of state service in probation and parole in Wisconsin, where he served as an agent and in various other direct-service positions, and Texas, where he was a full-time trainer of probation officers. Throughout his training career, Mr. Gingerich maintained contact with offenders as a cognitive skills coach and victim/offender mediator. He has been conducting training in evidence-based practices for many years throughout the United States (42 states), Canada, and abroad. Mr. Gingerich currently limits his training practice to motivational interviewing.

Melissa L. Meltzer, M.A., M.P.H., is a doctoral student at the University of Pennsylvania. She is the author of several journal articles and, most notably, "Going to the Other Side: An Analysis of Resilience Among Institutionalized Delinquent Youth," in *Child Victimization* (Civic Research Institute, 2005). Ms. Meltzer is presently working on a longitudinal study investigating the resilience of maltreated and incarcerated youth and serves as a member of the board of directors of the Harris County (Texas) STAR Drug Courts.

Made in the USA
Lexington, KY
30 November 2014